authentic

HOW TO MAKE A LIVING BY BEING YOURSELF

NEIL **CROFTS**

CAPSTONE

Copyright © Neil Crofts, 2003

The right of Neil Crofts to be identified as the author of this book has been asserted in accordance with the Copyright, Designs and Patents Act 1988

First published 2003 by
Capstone Publishing Limited (A Wiley Company)
The Atrium
Southern Gate
Chichester
West Sussex PO19 8SQ
http://www.wileyeurope.com

CIP catalogue records for this book are available from the British Library and the US Library of Congress

ISBN 1-84112-519-9

Typeset in 11/16 pt Adobe Garamond by Sparks Computer Solutions Ltd
http://www.sparks.co.uk

Printed and bound by TJ International Ltd, Padstow, Cornwall

Substantial discounts on bulk quantities of Capstone Books are available to corporations, professional associations and other organizations.
For details telephone John Wiley & Sons on (+44-1243-770441), fax (+44-1243-770571) or e-mail CorporateDevelopment@wiley.co.uk

For Benedi with love

To my wonderful wife without whom none of this would have been possible

Contents

Acknowledgements

With special thanks to Damon Leigh who made up for all that I failed to learn about English at school and has helped to turn pages of typing into a book. To Rob Best for being a true friend and collaborator in the big project. And also to Mark Allin and the team at Capstone who have made writing this book a wonderful experience.

Acknowledgements

Preface: Coming Out

Thinking about standing up and telling the world what you stand for is daunting. Actually doing it is frightening but the rewards are incredible. The whole of my previous career, perhaps the whole of my life I realize I have held back from being honest about my beliefs. I have held back for fear of ridicule. You know the sort of playground ridicule that comes from standing out in any small way.

Most of us seem to be coerced into conformity from a very early age by the dragon of normality. I call it a dragon not because it breathes fire or even because it is particularly nasty but because it is entirely fictitious.

There is no normal.

There is no right that is more right than your right.

Our careers and lives are so often blighted by our efforts to be what we THINK someone else wants us to be that we lose all confidence in our own judgement and instinct. When starting a business it is easy to feel that we must not be too controversial, as that will frighten customers away. Mostly we are tempted or persuaded to go with the bland, the grey and the anodyne just to make sure that we do not frighten people.

When I wrote the launch e-mail for Authentic Business (www.authenticbusiness.co.uk), I learned a lesson.

I wrote exactly what I thought. The only people whose opinion I asked were those I was sure would not try to water it down. I sent the e-mail almost as an act of defiance. I released the tension I have felt all of my life between what I believe and what I do by writing an e-mail and sending it to 4000 people.

The e-mail

How would it be if no one exploited any one or anything and no one felt exploited?

How would it be if everyone felt confident of their purpose and place in society?

How would it be if we all worked towards a common aim – happiness and quality of life for all, for example?

How would it be if companies collaborated to achieve this aim rather than competed for their own short-term gain?

How would it be if every business were authentic?

This paradigm shift, this revolution in consciousness, this replacement of the current orthodoxy is the aim of Authentic Business.

It will not be easy.

There will be many who will fight to protect the status quo.

Many of those who participate will face criticism and worse, they will also have to face their own uncertainty and confusion.

The rewards are joy, fulfilment, satisfaction and certainty.

Authentic Business facilitates this process by providing contacts, information, support and inspiration.

All you need to do to sign up for the solution to the tensions of our time is to read the articles and allow yourself to be inspired by them. Inspired to pass them on to friends, inspired to contact the authors and work with them, inspired to write articles yourself about your personal magic.

In this way working together we can create the world we want.

After I hit the send button I had what Douglas Adams would call a 'long dark tea-time of the soul' as I feared that my ranting had blown the whole idea and all of its credibility away.

Then the e-mails started to come in and this is what people wrote to me.

The responses

_____

Great to know you are around here, doing what you are doing.

_____

ok im intrigued

where do we go from here:)

----

love it

I really understand what you are trying to achieve now – well done!

I think there is a huge potential for Authentic Business, we are at the beginning of a huge wave of corporate and consumer change. Authentic Business is unique and it fits the current mood perfectly.

A big authentic thank you to you too for sending out my article. We have had lots of people contacting us via email in the past week. I can't say for sure where they've heard about us from, but I'm sure some of them have come from Authentic Business. I'd love to send you more articles if you're interested.

I love what you're doing and how you're doing it. Please add me to your newsletter list if you haven't already.

All the best with everything you're up to.

Having an uninspiring afternoon.

It is uninspiring no longer. And I haven't even had a chance to read the full articles.

Thank you.

Neil,

congratulations on the launch. I look forward to giving the articles my full attention.

— -

Had a bit more of a surf around the site since my last mail, spotted some friends, printed out an article, got inspired to write something myself …

Neil, this is really good stuff.

Yum.

— -

great stuff neil

— -

Thanks so much for this I will read the articles and also forward to my some of my friends who I know will appreciate the line of thought.

— -

Just to say I tried again today to visit the website and was successful. And impressed. Frustrated only that I cannot take the next several hours to read every bit. Know that I will return again soon and will advise others of this resource.

Best wishes with your new venture,

— -

I was so impressed with your mission/vision and what you have created … and all that AB stands for. Congratulations.

Thanks for the email. It all sounds interesting – well done and good luck!

It is comforting to know that there may be others out there like myself: questioning what running a business is really all about.

What a nice and encouraging project yours is! Congratulations and best wishes. And thank you for including me. I will be visiting your website shortly.

Authentic Business! Wow! Great things to come from that I am sure.

SOUNDS WONDERFUL – what are we supposed to do?

Thanks for your brilliant idea and the fact you have done something about it. I am starting a business, which is so much in line with what you are doing it feels like good news this morning to read about it.

These are all fantastic relevant words that resonate for many of us who aspire to set our own standards and live within our integrity. How do you plan on furthering your message? Where do you find the best response to these values? It is an endless realm for discussion and improvement. I wish you luck with it, many out there could benefit from the words below …

This is just a small sample of the supportive e-mails I was sent in response to that initial e-mail and I have not included any from friends. Of course there have also been a few who asked more or less politely, to be removed from the list, but the overriding response has been of support.

There are a number of lessons to be derived from this.

1 If you feel the tension, between who you are and what you do, give yourself the space and time to listen to what you are feeling, and understand it.

2 Think about it again and try articulating your thinking to people who might be sympathetic.

3 When you are ready, set your thinking free in the world, tell as many people as you can (by writing for Authentic Business for example) and see how the world responds to you.

4 Don't imagine that no one else cares. People have varying priorities. If you tell enough people you will find others who share yours.

5 Read this book.

How This Book Works

Authentic – How to Make a Living by Being Yourself is divided into four sections.

- *Section 1*. Sets the context about the society we live in and how it works. This is derived from the sense that I have been able to make out of a very confused picture, and borrows a great deal of wisdom from others.

- *Section 2*. Brings the focus down to a personal level and looks at what we can do to help ourselves and take control of our lives, how and why to make the decision to take control, and how to get started. This is based largely on my own experience, both personal and from working with others.

- *Section 3*. Describes how to actually make a living by being yourself.

- *Section 4*. Is a set of case studies of businesses that I believe to be authentic. They range from small fledglings to substantial businesses and prove beyond doubt, that as a way of making a living, authentic business is more successful in more dimensions than the dominant profit-centric business model.

Introduction

There is, I believe, a tension that many of us feel from an early age. The tension we feel is proportional to the difference between who we are and what we do.

All but a fortunate few of us are corralled and controlled through our childhood, education and youth to encourage us to fit in, to conform to an industrialized view of humanity where we are simply units in a process.

Unlike most other human societies, ours has no 'rites of passage' for adolescents to help them to understand who they are and what their natural talents are. In other societies they do have a rites of passage 'finding your medicine' as is practiced in many North American Indian societies or 'walkabout' which is the equivalent in Australian Aboriginal culture. In both examples young men are sent out into the bush alone to find out more about their strengths and character (rites of passage for young women are less common). Instead of this approach our society seeks to keep us distracted with TV, education, computer games and jobs, in the hope that once we 'grow up' we will realize the futility of resistance and 'fit in' to society.

- I use the term 'our society', to define all of those who live in the stratified, hierarchical society that we have created, as distinct from those who continue to live in tribal societies or who have escaped from ours.

- 'Fit in' seems increasingly like shorthand for giving up your identity, settling down, getting a job to pay off a mortgage and becoming a consumer. Our role is to consume addictive 'short-term hits of happiness' like soft drinks, cigarettes, sugar, alcohol, cars and fashion, all of which stop us from thinking too deeply about life and to be complicit in maintaining the charade that this is all that life is about.

As we 'go with the flow' the tension increases and leaves most people with two choices.

1   Stick with the programme and cover up the tension with addictions to short-term distractions.

2   Turn the life you have created upside down and go with your own flow.

In February 2001, I chose the latter. In amongst the fear, shock and apprehension there was also an extraordinary sense of liberation as I saw all of the props of my life disappearing.

It was in the aftermath of this, feeling happier, less tense and more connected to who I am than ever before, that the idea and the name for Authentic Business just popped into my head one day with absolute clarity and certainty.

I was sitting flicking through *Fast Company* and *Harvard Business Review* and wondering why I didn't read them. I realized that it was because the articles, largely about how to make more money, did not inspire me. So, I thought, why not just buy a business magazine that has inspiring articles about businesses that have some sort of positive purpose as well as profit? Well, after some thought and research, I realized that such a magazine did not exist.

The next step was to launch one. It was obviously going to be on-line because it combined a great deal of my previous experience in magazine publishing and Internet strategy. All I had to do was to work out a compelling and innovative business model that I could realize within the modest funds that I had available.

Although I have created Authentic Business myself I have not done it on my own. When I came up with the idea I started discussing it with people – both in person and by e-mail. By the time it went live there were probably around 250 people who had been involved in some way.

All of these people have been incredibly supportive and generous. I had top class business analysts help with the business plan. I had star PR help with the publicity. I had respected authors and copywriters help with the words. I had nearly 4000 e-mail addresses personally recommended to me. And the Web site was built on very generous terms.

Why was all this generosity forthcoming?

Because people are inspired by, believe in, and want to support the purpose to which Authentic Business is dedicated. That purpose is the liberation of business people from the mindless pursuit of profit, shareholder value and increasing bonuses for top executives, and its replacement with something that has meaning for them as individuals and makes a positive contribution to themselves, their community, our society and our environment.

This is why authentic businesses can be more successful – and successful in many more dimensions – than exploitative businesses. Everyone wants authentic businesses to succeed. And that is a big, big slice of competitive advantage.

Another Way to Look at the Society We Live In

Before we can begin to change ourselves we must understand the context we live in. How societal pressures have affected our lives and how the story we have been given to explain how our society got to be this way does not really add up.

Discovering, when I was about fifteen, that people, even those who are supposed to, did not often work for the good of society was a major revelation and shock to me. Since then I have been seeking to understand what is really going on and how we come to be this way. My conclusions are presented under the following headings.

- Dysfunctionality epidemic

- Indentured slavery

- Addiction to short-term hits of happiness

- Diagnosis

- Societal therapy

- The problem with decisions

- What is Authentic?

DYSFUNCTIONALITY EPIDEMIC

We are currently enduring the effects of a massive global pandemic that remains largely unrecognized and unspoken. This epidemic is not infectious but can be hereditary. It is probably because it is an epidemic of emotional problems rather than physical ones that it is so unrecognized.

This is an epidemic of dysfunctionality from which most of us suffer to a greater or lesser extent and because it can be hereditary a great many of us start our lives at a terrible disadvantage. A lucky few will escape it. Many will be able to recover after years of work and rehabilitation; many more will simply pass it on to their kids and keep suffering until they die.

It is not really our parents who are to blame. Its causes are by now thoroughly ingrained in our society, so that avoiding it might actually see you being regarded as rather abnormal. To understand this we need to look back at the history of our society and its foundations.

As a species we have been around in more or less our present form for about three million years depending on where you draw the lines. During virtually all of that time we have lived as tribal peoples. Although the shift started 10,000 years ago it is only in the last two or three thousand years, as our society has spread around the globe, that most of us have broken from our tribal roots and chosen a different way to live.

As tribal peoples, our ancestors spent millennia after millennia perfecting behaviours and methods that worked. Evolution has a simple brutality about it; behaviours that do not work lead to death. Only those who practise successful behaviours survive.

According to current historical thinking, around 10,000 years ago somewhere in the Middle East, a group of people came up with a new idea for running their society. They were not the first to try or the last but it has to be said that in some respects their model has been successful – for the moment. Of course 10,000 years is only a blip in terms of the three million years or so that humans have been around, a mere 0.0025% of our time on this planet.

The model that they chose involved a hierarchy where some people took control and decided that henceforth the other people would work for them. Control was ensured by frightening people with stories of dreadful enemies – some physical, some supernatural – and the occasional demonstration of their ruthlessness, both contrived and coincidental. Their masters convinced the people that they would protect them from the dreadful enemies if they paid a tax – initially in food, later in currency. A simple protection racket, which continues to be the basis of our taxation system to this day.

Evolution has a simple brutality about it; behaviours that do not work lead to death. Only those who practise successful behaviours survive.

At first, the job of being in control was easy enough. You left people largely to their own devices and if they failed to pay up you discretely beat up a few of them and blamed it on someone else to show how important your munificent protection was. However, after a while there was some need to legitimize the role of the masters and so those in charge took it upon themselves to design a society that would function and ensure their role as a ruling elite.

Ignoring millennia of evolutionary development, which had lead to highly sophisticated patterns of belief and organization and which sustainably regulated every aspect of life for nearly three million years, the new masters started from scratch.

They created the disciplines of law and order, medicine, education and all of the other facets of modern life.

Of particular relevance to the epidemic of dysfunctionality is the new way in which children came to be brought up and educated. In tribal times – and until fairly recently in much of Europe and what has become the US – children would be brought up by and with their parents. Within the tribe they had a multitude of mothers, fathers, grandparents, brothers and sisters. Every day would be a lesson in the real needs of life – sourcing and preparing food, creating and maintaining shelter, birthing siblings, and what to look for in a relationship. Life was tough but a child's upbringing prepared them for that. The weak ones died and their genes did not survive.

Tribal life is not utopia, but nor is it the primitive, impoverished torture that our society likes us to believe. Whatever you choose to believe about tribal ways one thing is clear: our society has done more damage to ourselves and our cohabitants on this planet in the last 10,000 years than tribal cultures did in the preceding three million. And if we want to learn to live sustainably then we have a great deal to learn from tribal cultures because they know how to do it.

There are a number of traits to tribal peoples behaviour – such as working with, rather than seeking to control, nature – that are common all over the world. We can only speculate about how they came to be common – maybe they spread from a single source or maybe these traits are so fundamental to survival that they have to develop for a society to survive. In any case, one of these traits, which has largely disappeared from our society, is the 'rites of passage' for adolescents mentioned in the introduction. Jesus Christ, Mohammed and Siddartha Gotama (the Buddha) are all supposed to have enjoyed the benefits of such empty time, free of distractions, to figure out what life was all about.

Far from including us in the life of our family and community and educating us in the essentials of life, far from giving us quiet, isolated soul time to discover who we are, upbringing today is largely outsourced by parents to others, and keeps children continually distracted as if to prevent them from learning how to think rather than helping them.

My own education was a prolonged and concerted attack on my individuality. From the beginning they dressed me up in a uniform so that my visual identity was compromised and then they began the long process of eroding my personality and, most importantly, my ability to think for myself and have confidence in those thoughts.

Fortunately for my ability to think for myself, the process left me so confused that in the end my schools largely gave up on me. I now discover that far from being unique this experience is almost uniform among the people that I work with. Including one who remembers the day they broke him and he developed a speech impediment.

In 1992, when he was still a teacher, US educational reformer and author of *The Underground History of American Education*, John Taylor Gatto, wrote an ironic essay entitled 'The Six-Lesson School Teacher', exposing the hidden curriculum behind our educational system. Here is an edited version.

- *Class*. Students must stay in the class where they belong. If things go well, the kids can't imagine themselves anywhere else; they envy and fear the better classes and have contempt for the dumber classes.

- *Caring*. I teach kids to turn on and off like a light switch. I demand that they become totally involved in my lessons, jumping up and down in their seats with anticipation, competing vigorously with each other for my favor. But when the bell rings I insist that they drop the work at once and proceed quickly to the next work station. Nothing important is ever finished in my class, nor in any other class I know of. The lesson of bells is that no work is worth finishing, so why care too deeply about anything?

- *Dependency*. Surrender your will to a predestined chain of command. Rights may be granted or withheld, by authority, without appeal. As a schoolteacher I intervene in many personal decisions, issuing a Pass for those I deem legitimate, or initiating a disciplinary confrontation for behavior that threatens my control. My judgments come thick and fast, because individuality is trying constantly to assert itself in my classroom. Individuality is a curse to all systems of classification, a contradiction of class theory.

- *Confidence*. I determine what curriculum you will study. (Rather, I enforce decisions transmitted by the people who pay me.) This power lets me separate good kids from bad kids instantly. Good kids do the tasks I appoint with a minimum of conflict and a decent show of enthusiasm. Of the millions of things of value to learn, I decide what few we have time for. The choices are mine. Curiosity has no important place in my work, only conformity.

Bad kids fight against this, of course, trying openly or covertly to make decisions for themselves about what they will learn. How can we allow that and survive as schoolteachers? Fortunately there are procedures to break the will of those who resist.

- *Conspicuousness*. Self-respect should depend on an observer's measure of your worth. My kids are constantly evaluated and judged. A monthly report, impressive in its precision, is sent into students' homes to spread approval or to mark exactly – down to a single percentage point – how dissatisfied with their children parents should be. Although some people might be surprised how little time or reflection goes into making up these records, the cumulative weight of the objective-seeming documents establishes a profile of defect which compels a child to arrive at a certain decisions about himself and his future based on the casual judgment of strangers.

- *Self-evaluation*. The staple of every major philosophical system that ever appeared on the planet – is never a factor in these things. The lesson of report cards, grades, and tests is that children should not trust themselves or their parents, but must rely on the evaluation of certified officials. People need to be told what they are worth.

- *Big Brother*. I keep each student under constant surveillance and so do my colleagues. There are no private spaces for children; there is no private time. Class change lasts 300 seconds to keep promiscuous fraternization at low levels. Students are encouraged to tattle on each other, even to tattle on their parents. Of course I encourage parents to file their own child's waywardness, too.

I assign 'homework' so that this surveillance extends into the household, where students might otherwise use the time to learn something unauthorized, perhaps from a father or mother, or by apprenticing to some wiser person in the neighbourhood.

Gatto's message is clear: the fact that our education is the way that it is is not an accident. As we are made to conform, our personality, individuality and self-confidence is driven out of us. Once we are sufficiently lacking in self-confidence we have to demean others to give ourselves a sense of importance. We will then pick on the slightest difference, weakness or failing so that we can build ourselves and diminish the other. And this behaviour is evident from playground, to office, to boardroom, to barracks, to hospital, to parliament.

As we are made to conform, our personality, individuality and self-confidence is driven out of us. Once we are sufficiently lacking in self-confidence we have to demean others to give ourselves a sense of importance.

Not only that, but the people we subcontract the education of our children to teach a bizarre mix of abstract subjects that have very little to do with real life. Where is the education about how to find your life partner (probably the most important decision you will take), where is the education about financial planning or nutrition?

More often than not our financial education is left to the banks and other financial institutions, which are hardly impartial; our nutritional education is left to Kellogg's and McDonald's who want us to consume their products; and our understanding of love and relationships is left to TV and films, which is at best overdramatic and creates unrealistic expectations of what love and romance are about.

Mass education started in the UK in 1818 with the first 'Ragged School' in Portsmouth, where children excluded from education because of their poverty were taught reading and writing, arithmetic and religion as well as cobbling (the founder was a cobbler), cooking and nature study. Over the next 20 years this genuinely philanthropic idea gathered funding and momentum until by 1844 the Ragged Schools Union was formed with over 200 schools.

The success of the Ragged Schools prompted the 1870 Education Act. This encouraged the election of local school boards in areas where other voluntary schools were insufficient. The school boards founded what were known as Board Schools and had powers to compel attendance, but these were seldom employed. The curriculum had a less strongly religious angle but still concentrated on teaching basic skills, mainly to children aged between five and ten years old. After this, children were expected to participate in some sort of vocational training such as apprenticeship.

The 1902 Education Act abolished the school boards and paved the way for the education system we have today. The aims of which were summarized paternalistically by its main author, the then Permanent Secretary for Education, Robert Morant: 'Teachers can endeavour by example and influence, aided by the sense of discipline which should pervade the school to implant habits of industry, self-control, courage and perseverance ... They can foster a strong respect for duty and respect for others, and in the playground develop the instinct for fair play to enable the children to become upright and useful members of the community.'

On the face of it this quote seems quite reasonable, but what do you see when you look through the political doublespeak and notice what is not there? There is no mention of the benefit to the individual, only to the community. There is no mention of identifying and nurturing talent, only implanting habits. This is a charter for conformity, and conformity has been the result.

The 1902 Education Act also introduced secondary education for the masses for the first time. The model that was used for secondary education was that employed in the elitist public schools and Oxbridge and so they imported a cut-down version for the poor kids. Latin, algebra, chemistry, biology, physics, English literature, mathematics and so on. Over the years it has been moderated and is now significantly more relevant to lives but it still has a long way to go.

The choice of subjects was not the only legacy of our education being forged in the furnace of the Industrial Revolution. Conformity was something that the Industrial Revolution was very much about. Factories churning out identical, mass-produced widgets for the first time found that a pliable and conforming workforce was important. The logical extension of industrialized manufacture was industrialized education. Teach all of the children the same things and forbid deviation and you end up with a conformist and obedient workforce.

As if to emphasise the separation from the reality, many Victorian schools were designed with windows that were too high for children to see out. After all, they didn't want kids to be distracted by reality.

All of this explains the dysfunctionality epidemic which, although it might be expressed in different ways – and have a multitude of consequences from Hitler and Saddam Hussein to agoraphobics who never leave home – it always seems to have its root in that lack of self-confidence implanted during childhood.

And those children who have their self-confidence taken away go on to be insecure adults and insecure parents. Not only that, but because their parents subcontracted their education and were not around enough when they were kids (because they were working in the factories/offices) the kids have no role-models for relation-ships, or for how to find the right partner.

And so the kids marry the wrong people and repeat the process again, thus creating the hereditary epidemic of dysfunctionality that is our society.

INDENTURED SLAVERY

When Westerners first discovered Tahiti in 1767 it was truly paradise. Plentiful breadfruit and a tropical climate combined to mean that primary needs of shelter and nourishment were taken care of, leaving the locals plenty of time to indulge in living. Tales of the happy, free-living islanders soon made their way back to England where the London Missionary Society was formed in 1795. Two years later the first missionaries arrived in Tahiti aboard a convict ship bound for Australia.

The missionaries were given a most hospitable welcome and made to feel very com-fortable, but after 14 years had still to make their first convert. However, they had managed to turn a local chief, Pomare, into an alcoholic. Their breakthrough came during a drinking session, when the missionaries promised guns to help Pomare win a battle with a more traditionally-armed neighbouring tribe if Pomare would assist in the enforced conversion of his people to Christianity.

The battle inevitably won, the conversion process got under way. Persistent unbelievers were put to death and a penal code was drawn up by the missionaries and enforced by the mission police. Wearing flowers, singing (other than hymns), surfing and dancing were declared illegal. Within a quarter of a century the process by which the native culture of Tahiti had been extinguished was exported to every corner of the Pacific, reducing the islanders to the level of the working class of Victorian England.

Debts are the shackles of our slavery. Twenty five years of indentured servitude to the bank forces us into having a job and leads us to believe that we have no alternative.

After their mass conversion it was hoped that the Tahitians might be induced to accept the benefits of civilization by putting them to work growing sugar cane. The enterprise failed the missionaries believing that 'a too bountiful nature … diminishes men's natural desire to work', ordered all the breadfruit trees to be cut down. By this time the population of Tahiti had been reduced by syphilis, tuberculosis, smallpox, and influenza from the 200,000 estimated by Cook to 18,000. After thirty years of missionary rule only 6000 remained. (Source: Lewis, N. (1988) *The Missionaries*, New York: McGraw-Hill)

We in the West like to imagine that we live in the 'free' world. I guess the term is relative. You have already read about how our upbringing damages our self-confidence and our intuition and you may well have asked yourself why would this happen? In whose interest is it to have a population that lacks self-confidence?

In the days before legal slavery was abolished there was a type of slavery known as indentured slavery. The indentured slave was contracted to their owner and worked in exchange for food and shelter. The contract was usually a fixed term and at the end of the contract the slave was free (but homeless and without food).

Today we have the mortgage (literally 'death pledge' – just think of that next time you see an advert for one), and other debts coupled with high prices for houses – one of our most basic human needs after food and drink – to ensure our servitude to the system.

High prices for housing might be counter-productive for those leaving education of course because the high prices might encourage them to look for alternatives to buying or renting a house. So, we have student loans, sold vigorously by the banks, to ensure that as many of us as possible are locked into the system as early as possible.

I use the term 'the system' because although I do not see it as a conspiracy I believe that our society has evolved a self-perpetuating social, economic and political system which is very hard to challenge.

There is nothing real about the value of property. It is an illusion maintained by the insidious combination of the basic need for shelter and the way in which we are loaned money to buy it. Banks and other lenders incentivise their sales staff with short-term targets for selling more total value of mortgages, per month or per quarter. At the same time, completely separate departments typically run targets for minimizing defaults on payments, debt collection and managing repossessions. The result is that although the selling department do take affordability into consideration it is not what motivates them and they are constantly trying to lend more money to more and more people. As long as they have the deeds for the property to secure it, they do not really care as they lend four, five and even six times income.

Imagine what the price of property would be if banks would only lend half your annual salary rather than greater multiples of salary. Of course, now that we are here we cannot go back, going back would throw so many people into negative equity that it is not going to happen. So we continue to collude with the system most of us without the self-confidence to challenge it or to try alternative paths.

Debts are the shackles of our slavery. Twenty five years of indentured servitude to the bank forces us into having a job and leads us to believe that we have no alternative. Until recently there really were very few alternatives, since banks were reluctant to lend to people who could not demonstrate a regular salary. Since the disappearance of the 'job for life' banks have now become far more willing to lend to the self-employed and freelancers giving far more flexibility than previously existed.

It is not just the fragile value of our assets that persuade us to collude with the system. It is also our education and conditioning to the system and the largely manufactured fear of threats from disease, crime, war, terrorism and, worst of all, loss of jobs which commit us to it. Governments and the media propagate the fear whether it is real or imagined. In the last few years, fear of crime in the UK and the US has risen while actual crime levels have fallen; most of the time it is only the perception of threat that is important not its execution.

It is in the interests of the system to have a population that will willingly submit itself to such long-term service. Our time is used to generate income most of which is shared between the government as tax, which is based on the protection racket principles discussed above, and the bank. What is left is used up in feeding and other necessities and a little bit left over to pay to distract us from the truth of our situation.

There are alternatives of course; this is the 'free' world after all. You might be one of the fortunate few who can pay for your home outright. Perhaps this is because you have enough money or perhaps because the home you choose is cheap enough, like living in a caravan, houseboat or somewhere cheaper.

If you choose an alternative to the indentured slavery model you need to be prepared to be treated as an outcast. Our society is so wrapped up in our commitment to the system that we regard those who choose not to participate as lesser people. This is more a conditioned reaction based on John Gatto's 'class' lesson discussed earlier, than a considered response.

We have spent our entire lives being conditioned by the media and our education to believe that our system is the only true way. Alternatives are to be feared – conveniently they form part of the threat that we need to pay to be protected from.

In the UK, as recently as the late 1980s, we have seen brutal police repression of people seeking an alternative lifestyle in the 'Battle of the Beanfield'. Police physically attacked a convoy of travellers in their homes who they believed were making their way to Stonehenge to celebrate midsummer. At the time travellers were the media's fashionable 'threat to civilization' in the UK – where are they now? Do they still exist and are no longer a threat to society or were they coerced into conformity? In 2003 the threat to society is asylum seekers – who will it be next year?

In Gloucestershire in the UK, sculptor Jack Everett and his family have chosen an ultra-low-impact lifestyle and built their house in some woodland that they own. They have lived there for eighteen years without electricity or running water and make all that they need through selling sculptures. In 2001 they fought and lost a court battle with their local council who evicted them because their home was built without planning consent.

Clearly it would have been better if they had built the house with planning consent in the first place – except that getting planning permission for anything out of the ordinary is next to impossible in the UK. However, the council's argument is that if these people are allowed to 'get away with it' then everyone will want to.

I find it hard to imagine that all of our woodland is in imminent danger of people buying it up to build homes with no running water or electricity, but how bad would it be if this happened? More very low impact homes would help to balance up the impact of 'normal' housing. What is tragic is that, instead of choosing to learn from these situations and understand what this family's innovation may have to offer, our society just rejects it.

An alternative would be to encourage self-building communities for people who would rather not be part of the system. There are, of course, communities who do take care of themselves. The Amish of Pennsylvania continue to collaborate to build their own homes. Christiania in Copenhagen, Denmark and Findhorn in Scotland are examples of self-built communities. Instead of these ideas being regarded as interesting options by the mainstream, we are wedded to a monoculture, which drives us towards conformity rather than embracing and celebrating diversity.

In the UK, with the exception of the Chinese, we have even sought to diminish the cultural heritage of our immigrants, insisting that they conform to some idea of 'Englishness'. Imagine if we had learned from the Chinese lesson. Imagine if Southall were recognized and promoted as London's Delhi or Brixton as an eastern outpost of the West Indies.

All over the world Chinese communities have banded together and celebrated their culture. They have taken over areas of major cities and 'branded' them. They install elaborate symbolic gates and adjust architecture. The shops sell Chinese goods, the restaurants are all Chinese, there are Chinese bookshops, doctors, supermarkets and so on. Visitors are welcome and there is a special feeling about the whole Chinatown area that contributes to the host city.

Sadly, conformity and 'integration' is more common both for communities and individuals. Through the 'carrot' of having somewhere to live and the 'stick' of avoiding exclusion and poverty, we are coerced into participating in the system. For most of us this means having a job. And for most of us having a job means spending literally the best part of our day away from the homes that we are working hard to pay for, and away from our loved ones. If you were designing our society from scratch would you want it to be this way?

The self-serving futility of the system does not end there. For most of us, the jobs that we do serve little truly useful purpose for ourselves or our cohabitants on this planet; and for many, both the work and the travel it involves is simply about turning finite and diminishing resources into more pollution. Not just the incidental pollution that is a by-product of the work that we do but very often the product itself is pollution both of people's lives and of the planet.

What I mean by pollution here is that these things pollute people's lives and diminish their potential as a result. Things like short-lived fashion items, trash media, exploitative financial products, trashy souvenirs and gifts and bad food. They are created simply to redistribute wealth towards the owners of the business and are not to do with enhancing the lives of their purchasers.

We buy them not to enhance our lives but to compensate, in some way, for the disappointment we feel in the life we are living and to make us feel that it is all worth something. The emptiness that indentured slavery makes us feel ensures that we are susceptible to becoming addicted to short-term hits of happiness.

ADDICTION TO SHORT-TERM HITS OF HAPPINESS

At some level we are all simply seeking to be happy. For most of us, if we paraphrase Maslow's hierarchy (see detailed description in 'What is Authentic?' on p. 25), happiness includes four basic elements: comfort, security, love and understanding. If we had all of these most of the time we could probably say that we were happy.

In the society in which we live comfort comes at a price. Our feeling of security is constantly undermined by news of recession/redundancy, accidents, crime, war and terrorism. Love is hard to find or understand for many with no personal loving role-models to aspire to. And understanding our complex and contrary world is a real challenge.

Happiness seems like the end of the rainbow – something you can see and vaguely understand but never truly experience. We do feel moments of happiness, and even euphoria, when we buy ourselves some new thing or are praised by our boss, but these are fleeting and usually attached to events or things. In this way we develop an understanding that happiness is external, that it comes from the outside.

This then leads to a constant search for happiness in external events or objects. Such happiness can only ever be short-lived (and perhaps relatively shallow) so we need to constantly find new hits of happiness. It becomes an addiction; we are addicted to these hits like any addict always searching for their next dose. Like any addiction it turns into a spiral of diminishing returns. The dosage of things or events needs to be stronger to get the same thrill and, in the end, most things are a disappointment, rarely living up to the expectations.

The system works to distract us from thinking too deeply about these disappointments. We are constantly told that the next thing, the next event will really do it for us. We even convince ourselves that we really like the latest thing for a while, but denial is part of the nature of addiction.

Addiction is usually a substitute for some crucial, but unidentified, element missing from our lives. As we have seen, we are first convinced to conform by having our self-confidence eroded. Then, once we have lost the confidence to change things we are obliged by the system of indentured slavery to participate in a world of jobs where many of us spend a good deal of time not being truly happy.

We have to justify the commitment of time, emotion and energy that we put into earning an income, beyond just paying for a home and food. So it can feel important to buy ourselves treats with the money that we earn and, if we don't earn enough, we will borrow to pay for them, further indebting ourselves to the system.

On its own, this is not enough to explain the religion of consumerism that, for many people requires frequent pilgrimages to a supermarket, mall or other place of worship, with their great vaulted ceilings and long aisles. Here we part with our hard-earned cash as donations exchanged for the icons of our modern religion, branded goods.

There is a continuum that runs from Christ to cocaine: of externalizing responsibility for our own happiness to others, be they products or people. This is another consequence of the destruction of our self-confidence during childhood. Many of us, especially in the West, lack the confidence to seek our happiness from within and, wrapped up as we are in trying to keep up with the mortgage payments by doing a job which has little real meaning for us, we look outside for comfort and meaning.

This lack of spiritual fulfilment has created the demand side of consumerism where we seek happiness in some chocolate, a new coat, a new car or whatever. That demand is both fuelled and fulfilled by companies who use the dependence that they create to help them to channel wealth towards their owners and senior executives.

The systems of capitalism and public stock markets have turned the largest of these companies into massive financial redistribution machines. These machines consume natural resources, human energy and emotion in order to move money from the poorer to the richer. As a by-product, they turn out goods to feed our addiction that are, in turn, hyped by advertising. Poor workers are exploited to make cheap mass-produced products for consumption by the masses. The profits from these transactions find their way to the richest 1 or 2% of the people in the world, not to the other 98%.

We have developed a way of justifying all of this, as though it is somehow inevitable and that we do not really have a choice, either as individuals or as a society. 'That's life', we say, but deep down somewhere we know that there is more to life than jobs, mortgages and consumer goods. Unfortunately, because of our conditioning to conform we find it very hard to be honest about what we really want from life, or from other people.

Damon, who helped me with the writing of this book wrote this while he was reading through the drafts:

> 'I've recently realized something about myself. The myth of ownership – if I buy this my life will be better – underpins consumerism and all advertising. When the myth shatters, temporarily, we're left with empty disappointment of owning something, being that much worse off financially, yet nothing has really changed. I realized recently, on a shopping trip, that I now have that process compressed into seconds! I see something and the (puny!) consumer in me says "ooh, that's nice!" Then I go pick it up, and instantly have the flash-forward to the empty disappointment stage. I don't so much put the object back as drop it like a hot potato! It's now hard for me to buy stuff, even as presents, because I seem to be able to sense the empty disappointment that the receiver will get from it, too.'

DIAGNOSIS

You know if you are dysfunctional, if you are working in indentured slavery or if you are addicted to short-term hits of happiness. You might not use those terms but you know. If you feel that you are bounced around by events rather than in control of your life; if you feel that you are trapped and there is nothing you can do about it; if you feel that you lack confidence in yourself and are unable to be decisive; if you do not trust your intuition but prefer to base decisions and choices on what you believe is rational evidence; if you find it hard to trust others and are overcritical of the behaviour of people close to you – if you recognize any of these, take note! These are all signs that your self-confidence has been damaged. By learning to trust yourself and hear and believe your intuition you could liberate yourself and realize your true potential.

For ideas on how to achieve this for yourself and for the rest of the world, read on.

SOCIETAL THERAPY

'A nation that fails to learn the lessons of history is destined to repeat it.'

Winston Churchill

Churchill might have been talking about individuals as much as about nations. Life seems to have an extraordinary way of teaching us lessons. The first nudge is usually quite minor, if you are alert you will spot it and, if you are conscious enough, you will do something about it. If you fail to see it the ensuing nudges will get progressively bigger and more demanding of attention. Eventually it will be like having a billboard right in front of you with ten metre high letters in lurid orange.

There is a film about this called *Groundhog Day*. The first time I saw it I thought it was just a charming romantic comedy. Later, I realized that it contains a valuable lesson: in the film Bill Murray is destined to repeat his least favourite day until he gets it right.

As this is true for individuals, so it is also true for nations and civilizations, the only differences being those of scale. As a society we are now seeing the ten metres high letters on the billboard and we really have to take notice.

Therapy is a process of uncovering and exploring these lessons to see how they influence the present. This process can be a wonderful experience and can lead to all sorts of revelations and understanding about oneself. Perhaps it is time that we took on board a little societal therapy so that we can understand where we are going wrong and what to do about it.

One of frequent factors in the fall of civilizations is that the people become distracted by decadence and are not able to resolve the terminal issues that face them.

No society based on hierarchy and exploitation has survived for long. We may like to see ourselves as the inheritors of the Roman and Greek civilizations but we are not – the Roman and the Greek empires both fell and their civilizations with them. We have learned some things from our forbears but we have forgotten more.

Every other civilization since the first one has come to an end – what makes us think that ours is special?

One of frequent factors in the fall of civilizations is that the people become distracted by decadence and are not able to resolve the terminal issues that face them. The direct cause may be military takeover, or a damaged ecology leading to a lack of resources, but if the population is not alert to the issues they will not be able to make the changes necessary to survive.

Our society has a burning need to move beyond the trivial distraction of our population and to move to a more meaningful way of living. The solution lies not with government, not with protest or with revolution, but with every single decision that we, the citizens of the world, make.

THE PROBLEM WITH DECISIONS

Most of the big problems that we face as inhabitants of this finite planet are the consequence of decisions made by people in our society. Before globalization the finite nature of the planet did not seem like a problem since there were always new territories to conquer and exploit. Now that there are no further territories the only solution within that mindset is to 'conquer' space. The conclusion that you have to draw from this is that we are not terribly good at making decisions either as individuals or as a society. So why, after all this time, are we still so bad at making decisions?

Most of us like to believe that we are taking rational decisions. The problem with what we think of as rational decisions is that they are not actually rational. For rational decisions to really work they would need to take account of all of the data. And taking account of all of the data is not possible since you cannot even access all of the existing data, let alone the future data.

Most of the poor decisions we take are, in fact, dysfunctional emotional decisions justified and influenced by carefully selected data. The reason for this is, once again, our lack of self-confidence. Our upbringing has taught us not to trust our emotions or intuition and so we are unable to trust our emotions to help us to take balanced decisions using both our rational and emotional powers.

In order to take balanced decisions we need to understand and trust ourselves, we need to be authentic and we need to be working in areas with which we are emotionally connected. In my work I hear a good deal of talk of business managers needing to have emotional intelligence and hiring training companies and consultants to give it to them.

The difficulty for companies is that unless the business managers can be emotionally connected to the work they do the greatest effect that these consultants and training companies have is that their emotionally awakened students leave the company (that paid for the training) in search of emotional connection and meaning.

In the 'rational' world of big business and politics taking decisions based on or even including belief, feeling and emotion is tantamount to admitting that you have lost your mind and are ready to resign. We are intimidated into accepting the rule of the rational by our lack of sufficient confidence to say simply 'because I believe in it'. In the run up to the second Gulf War, British Prime Minister Tony Blair's use of belief as his final line of defence in justifying the war was effective partly because it is so unusual, but it seems likely that this was an emotional cover-up for some highly rational and politically unpopular decision making.

The irony, of course, is that most big businesses and political ideologies nominally represented by corporations and political parties started out with passionately held beliefs, but with far less rational evidence than they like to employ today. The beliefs of the founders were sold out as the organization grew and became more 'professional'.

If we, as a society, are to overcome our present difficulties of dysfunctionality, indentured slavery and addiction to distraction before they lead to really significant disruption to both our civilization and to our cohabitants on this planet, we need to understand how to take decisions that are both in touch with ourselves and in touch with the wider world context to which they relate.

The only way we can do this is by learning to trust ourselves and learning to take decisions with an open mind and an open heart, based both on the rational evidence and on being able to listen to and trust our intuition. In a word, by being 'authentic'.

WHAT IS AUTHENTIC?

Our experience of life and the world around us is based exclusively on what we sense, and our interpretation of those inputs.

There are no truly objective facts on which to base anything – everything we see, everything we feel, everything we know is based on our subjective interpretation of information fed to us by our senses.

In June 2000 I was first on the scene at a fatal motorbike accident. I knew clearly what I had seen, and yet when I came to give evidence to the investigating policeman, who had constructed a view based on all of the witness's accounts, it differed from mine in most important details.

Understanding that there is no objective reality, there is no single truth, that no one is actually right is hugely liberating.

The world in which you live is your world, one constructed by your mind in order to make sense of what is going on outside it.

This wisdom exists in Buddhism, in existentialist philosophy, in Taoism and many other teachings from around the world; it is not new or unique.

Our confidence in our interpretation is confused by events in our childhood, perceived pressure from others, social convention, marketing messages and chemical changes in our bodies.

Talking with colleagues, clients, friends, reading history or watching movies or dramas we constantly see how internal confusion leads to damaging misjudgement.

So how can we begin to trust ourselves?

It is easy to understand the way trust develops. Animal trainers call it positive reinforcement. An action or instruction is followed by a predictable response. A dog is instructed to sit, the dog sits, the instructor praises the dog. The dog learns that sitting when instructed results in praise.

However, much of our experience of life and therefore ourselves is not like that. Childhood experiences, jobs, behaviour of government and experience of goods and services we buy are filled with disappointments. We learn that the world and, crucially, our interpretation of it, is not predictable or trustworthy.

If the world we experience is exclusively about our interpretation of events, and trust is about predictability of reaction, it follows that if we can ensure that at least our own reactions are predictable we can begin to trust ourselves.

The problem is that most of us are brought up to believe that others might have a more real interpretation of the world than we do. This results in our learning not to trust, or very often even listen to, our own instincts.

How many of us choose to eat food, go to parties, accept jobs or even marry while feeling a sense of unease, but not listening to it or believing we can do anything about it?

It doesn't need to be like this.

We can decide to listen to our instincts, trust them and act on them. Being honest with ourselves seems hard to start with – we have years of conditioning to break – but once we make the leap it is harder still to be dishonest with ourselves.

Being honest with yourself is about making every decision and choice consciously and explicitly, even if it seems difficult, rather than allowing yourself to be swept along by events.

Once we start to be honest with ourselves, we can start to trust ourselves, which gives us more confidence in every situation. This is the confidence of authenticity.

So how can authentic businesses help?

Like it or not, business is currently the main driver of our society. About half of the largest economic units in the world are corporations, dwarfing many countries in terms of value of transactions. Corporations lobby and sponsor elected governments to reduce the chances that anti-business legislation is enacted. Big business has driven the formation of the World Trade Organization – an unelected body, which has developed legal powers that oblige participating governments to act in the interest of business, even when it is against the wishes of the population that elected them. This ensures that concepts like the right of business to make a profit and the importance of 'shareholder value' as a driver for business are largely unquestioned and are accorded a priority above many social and environmental issues.

Over the last thousand years we have been through phases of ascendancy:

- *the religious*, during much of the Middle Ages and into the Reformation;

- *the martial*, during the Roman and Napoleonic eras where military thinking and power prevailed; and

- *the political*, during the time of the British Empire (where religion was used for largely political ends) and the communist era.

Throughout the 20th century, business and capitalism grew in influence until, after the fall of communism, it took over as the most influential force in our society.

Over the same period as the practice of business matured it shed much of the idealism of earlier business people such as Cadbury, who built the village of Bournville to house workers and set up a trust to maintain it because he believed that if workers were happy they would be more motivated. Idealism was replaced with rationalism. Business has become largely about profit and shareholder value, and decision-making processes are dominated by these narrow priorities.

'Professional' business people (too often men) came to believe that it was possible to make rational, as opposed to balanced, emotional and rational, decisions. Emotion came to be suppressed under the blanket of research, data and consultants that is used to insure managers and leaders against the consequences of taking decisions.

In a society dominated by rationalists, idealists are marginalized through education, media, business, infrastructure and all of the other tools always deployed by defenders of an increasingly precarious status quo. The same thing happened and happens with Flat-Earthers, Darwinists and Geo-centrists.

In an industrial society an ill-educated populace can be effectively exploited to perform mechanistic operations. But development creates a self-sustaining cycle where demand for better lifestyle creates demand for better education. This cycle creates an increasing tension as the demands of the work fail to live up to the expectations created by the education.

The paradigm shift occurs when the tension of the expectations exceeds the cohesion of the limitations.

As society becomes more affluent we move up Maslow's pyramid (see below). We start with the basics of food, water and shelter, moving on to establish our safety and security, to realizing needs of belonging and love, to esteem and recognition needs, then to a need to understand our selves and our world, to aesthetic needs for beauty and finally to self-actualization and, possibly, transcendence. Eventually, through this process, we arrive at a point where enough of us recognize our need

to understand and realize our own potential and it becomes clear that helping big corporations to become bigger and exploit better fails to deliver that for us.

At that point we discover the need for a new model for business. A model that delivers on our needs for self-actualization. A model for business that is about our own true purpose. That is Authentic Business.

What Are You Going To Do About It?

2

'Our deepest fear is that we are powerful beyond measure. It is our light not our darkness, that most frightens us. We ask ourselves who am I to be brilliant, gorgeous, talented, fabulous? Actually, who are you not to be? You are a child of the Earth. Your playing small does not serve the world. There's nothing enlightened about shrinking so that other people won't feel insecure around you. We are all meant to shine, as children do ... And as we let our own light shine, we unconsciously give other people permission to do the same. As we are liberated from our own fear, our presence automatically liberates others.'

Marianne Williamson

This is your opportunity. You can decide right now whether you want to want to be brilliant, gorgeous, talented, fabulous, or not. If you decide not to, please close this book right now and give it to someone else who might decide to go for it and have no regrets or thoughts of what might have been. You are free to choose to continue as you are and be content with that.

If you do decide you want to face the challenge and to know more, we are going to go on a journey. Firstly we will look at four preparations and then eight actions to do something about it:

- Preparation 1: To tell the truth

- Preparation 2: Perception and reality

- Preparation 3: Finding your 'natural language'

- Preparation 4: What is my point in life?

- Action 1: Eating your energy

- Action 2: Exercise your mind

- Action 3: Taking control of your life

- Action 4: Avoiding distraction and inspiring change

- Action 5: Editing your address book

- Action 6: Changing habits

- Action 7: Making your plan

- Action 8: Coming out and being yourself

PREPARATION 1: TO TELL THE TRUTH

As children we are often told not to lie but we are seldom taught how to tell the truth. Not only that, but many of our teachers, parents, TV personalities and politicians are role-models of dishonesty. It is not that these role-models lie or are particularly dishonest, but that, from the point of view of an innocent child trying to make sense of the world in a very literal way, any discrepancy between words and deeds is very confusing.

The truth is, of course, a rather abstract concept. It is intensely personal, which makes it rather difficult for anyone else to know whether you are telling it or not. Which is where the problems start.

The only person who knows if you are telling the truth is you. Unless you are prepared to be the one who keeps an eye on it there is rarely any direct comeback on you for not telling the truth and so it often seems easier to lie.

As children we are often told not to lie but we are seldom taught how to tell the truth.

An even more common and insidious dishonesty is the dishonesty of silence, where we fail to mention crucial truths often to those closest to us. I was in a relationship that was not founded on honesty for a long time, there was so much that went unsaid. We have said it now. It only took an evening, but not saying it for all of those years certainly contributed to our separation.

In reality, telling the truth is similar to lying in that it is just about technique. If you think about whatever you have to say, there is an honest way to say it that will not cause needless pain. Most of us learn an adversarial system where we feel we need to enter conversations already knowing the outcome and that the purpose of the conversation is to bring our interlocutor around to our point of view. It turns out that it is far easier and more honest to enter into conversations unprepared and allow a new solution to emerge through collaboration rather than confrontation. Frequently this means not imagining you already know the answer, but asking questions and discovering that a truth emerges that is quite different to the one you may have been trying to hide.

Unsurprisingly, for many of us, it is not quite as simple as that. Many of us started lying at an early age. Lets take a typical parents lesson to their children in lying.

The threat. If you do that one more time I will … The problem here is that the threat is often hard for the parent to carry out and so they don't. The child, instead of learning not to do the thing in question, learns that their parents do not always tell the truth.

It is not just parents who teach us how to lie – teachers, TV advertising (remember the first time you persuaded your parents to buy you something you saw advertised on TV and were disappointed by it?) and later employers and politicians are all influential in teaching us dishonesty.

So what does telling the truth involve? And do we really want to anyway?

The first person that we need to learn to be honest with is ourselves. Until we can trust ourselves there is little chance of us being honest with others. We need to understand the myths that we create for ourselves to justifying doing things or not doing things.

Many of us create one or more alter egos behind which we live most of the time. These alter egos are defined by second guessing how we think others want us to behave. We spend much of our time flipping between our work selves, our home selves and, if we are lucky, our real selves.

All of this sucks away at our energy and leaves us confused, unhappy and prey to the distractions of consumerism. It becomes easy for marketers to persuade us that we are too weak to resist temptations and that we will be happy if we buy that soft drink, beer, make-up, camera, car, whatever.

By learning to be honest with ourselves we create possibility to be authentic and free up all of that energy we were previously using to maintain our alter egos. Unfortunately this is as difficult as it sounds. Many of us have spent years developing convincing alter egos and sub personalities that behave in particular ways with particular people and in particular situations. Persuading yourself to come clean is hard.

Once you have learned to be honest with yourself you will find it pays off in every area. Life and relationships become easier. Which brings us to the next person you need to be honest with – your significant other.

A great many relationships are based on unspoken truths, exaggerations and out-right lies. These relationships develop a set of unwritten and unspoken rules of what is and is not discussed and done. Although our role-models, of parents, TV and movie relationships, seldom reveal it, our significant relationships must ideally be based on unconditional reciprocal love if they are to be fulfilling for both parties.

Unconditional reciprocal love.

Nothing else is acceptable if you want to be your authentic self and to be all that you can be.

In the summer of 2000 I commissioned a training session called Authentic Leadership for my team at Razorfish. The session was run by Paul Wielgus, a sublime facilitator of personal development sessions. Thirty-five business strategists from all over Europe and North America discussed authentic leaders and authenticity. We delved into ourselves, in some cases for the first time. Nine months later a third of the participants had separated from the partners and spouses we had at the time.

If the relationship you have is not the right one and cannot be made to be right you must act and act soon. To be your authentic self you can only be with someone who loves you for who you truly are and not someone for whom you have to be one of your alter ego personalities.

Although marriage vows in most of Europe have moved on to some extent, they still have their basis in a promise to God or state. To have an authentic relationship you need something which is very much team based and is a commitment you make to each other. Whether or not you choose to get married and whether or not you choose to make a commitment to God, I think it is worth making this kind of commitment to one another, publicly or privately. This is the commitment that I wrote for the relationship we have now and we used for our marriage. It may be helpful to see if you and your partner can make such a commitment to one another.

- To share in unconditional love and support

- To live in absolute integrity and authenticity

- To enjoy mutual challenge and inspiration

- To embrace constant personal change and development

- To give unequivocal space alongside absolute security

If you cannot make this kind of commitment to each other over the long term you may be able to agree with one another that you would be better off not being together.

If you are in this situation this is perhaps the toughest part of coming out and being honest with yourself. You may have spent years developing a life and a lifestyle, which would all be thrown away by taking this step. All I can say is that I did it and, although it was probably not handled perfectly, and certainly generated a great deal of anguish for four people, it was better in the long run for all concerned because neither of the two relationships that were broken up were founded on honesty.

PREPARATION 2: PERCEPTION AND REALITY

'How do you define real? If you are talking about what you can feel, what you can smell, what you can taste and see then real is simply electrical signals interpreted by your brain.'

Morpheus – The Matrix

As was mentioned in the first section, reality is an intensely personal thing. Our senses perceive sound, light, texture, taste, odour, colour but we have absolutely no way of knowing whether your experience of A minor, dark, rough, strawberry, Chanel no 5, or blue is the same as mine or not. We absorb information through our senses, which our mind then filters and interprets.

The way we interpret information is affected by all sorts of things – circumstance, mood, age, gender, past experience. But, crucially, it is conditioned by belief. There are many people in the world who will regard the ideas in this book as ridiculous or dangerous or will not even notice them. This is because the ideas simply do not fit within their current belief system.

Remember there was a time when people were killed for saying that the Earth revolved around the sun and that it was round. The idea that we were descended from apes was so heretical that it took Charles Darwin years to pluck up the courage to tell us. People find it extremely hard to have their fundamental beliefs altered and, given such radical revelations of the not-so-distant past, who would bet that our current world-view is the only true one?

Perhaps we can go further. Maybe my perception that the world is dangerous and dysfunctional is only a reflection of my own state of mind. Maybe, once I complete my journey and reach peace or nirvana or transcendence or whatever you like to call it, the world (or my experience of it) will resolve to a happy heavenly place.

Certainly, you perceive the world differently to the way I do. Perhaps you already think it is an entirely safe and happy place and wonder what on earth I am on about.

How can you tell the difference between what is real and what is imagined?

Our beliefs derive from our experiences and our conditioning. If your beliefs are not aligned with your natural language (see Preparation 3: Finding your 'natural language') you are likely to have a distorted idea of their value to the world and of your own capability. So the next step is to adjust your world-view to accommodate your natural language.

Once you begin to understand your natural languages you may need to be prepared to rethink your world-view. To do this you will first need to understand what your world-view is and where it comes from. Your world-view is how you see yourself, society and your place in it.

Ask yourself these questions and then ask why you answered that way and what other answers there could be.

- How would it be if you really did control events?

- Do you think that you have the choice about how you direct your energy?

- Why do we consistently fail to eradicate poverty?

- What motivates the choices that are made in the world?

- What is control?

- What is success?

- How would it be if we did not live in a hierarchy?

In many cases our conditioning has lead us to believe that our natural language is not valuable or important. Open your mind to the possibility that your unique brilliance is valuable to the rest of the world and therefore to you. This will lead you to asking: what is my natural language?

PREPARATION 3: FINDING YOUR 'NATURAL LANGUAGE'

The good news is that you know what your natural language is. The bad news is that it may be very well hidden.

Firstly, what do we mean by natural language? Language is about communication. Your natural language is the way that you most easily communicate with your surroundings. Your natural language could take almost any form and you will have more than one.

For many of us our natural language is buried because during our education we were obliged to learn a number of other languages regardless of whether they had any meaning for us personally or not. For most of us, our natural language was not included in our education and most of us were persuaded to quietly forget about it.

We hear about people being described as 'gifted'. In reality we are all gifted. In the case of the people being described as gifted their natural language happened to coincide with one of the languages they were being taught at that time. It happened to be spotted by someone and supported.

In 2002 the BBC in the UK screened a TV show called *Fame Academy*. Out of thousands of applicants a lucky few were selected for ten weeks of intensive coaching and mentoring in their natural language of singing and performing. The students who survived the first selection rounds had their lives changed and went from being good singers to being outstanding performers of tremendous character and confidence.

For the rest of us we are told, by implication, that we are not gifted. This is not true. You are gifted. All you need is to identify your natural language and to go with your flow rather than the flow imposed by society.

Imagine if, rather than being the exception, the level of coaching seen in *Fame Academy* was available to everyone. Imagine if, instead of being distracted by years of indoctrination, we were given the space to discover our natural language, and then offered intensive support and coaching.

Finding your natural language is about identifying the languages you intuitively understand. At some level you know what they are; it may just be a question of looking at the things you find easiest to do or the things you dream of doing. This is your opportunity and your responsibility. If you wait for someone else to do if for you, it simply will not happen.

Finding your natural language is about identifying the languages you intuitively understand. The search needs to focus on the inside not on the outside; in the same way that many tribal cultures have rites of passage that involves sending adolescents out into the wilderness to be on their own without distraction. In our society, finding any time without distraction can be quite a challenge in itself.

I believe that our natural language is strong within us and will surface if we give it a chance. If you consciously search for it, you will be able to find it. Whatever you are doing, be conscious of how you feel, be conscious of the tension you are feeling, and focus in on the areas where you feel less tension and feel more at peace with yourself.

We are conditioned to feel that introspection is a rather selfish and anti-social thing to be doing. To make time for empty contemplation is a real challenge. The time I do most of my contemplation is while I am out cycling. I spent seven years commuting by bike across London for about an hour each way. I also went on long training rides of three hours or more. This is intensely valuable thinking time with the potential of few distractions.

Of course, cycling is not for everyone. Meditation is highly recommended by some, others have found Buddhist chanting an enormous help. Other options are walking, running or swimming. There are any number of techniques. All you have to is to find one that suits you. The vital, and yet most difficult thing is to make time. I made the time by having cycling as part of my daily schedule. As with everything in life it is about priorities. You need to decide what is important in your life and focus on this, while doing less of what is not important.

While you are working to understand your natural languages you need to find wise people with whom you can discuss what you are feeling and learning. The natural languages you identify could take many forms. I happen to be comfortable with exploring, understanding and articulating. This makes me good at technical subjects like making and fixing things, cooking, navigation, understanding people and society. None of this was fostered or supported during my education, in spite of the wide range of schools I sampled.

In my work I find that a focus on inspiration and discussion is effective for most people given enough time. However, if you feel particularly confused or have been traumatized even in what may seem to be a very minor way during your childhood you may have some more work to do.

Like the world's wisdom, help and assistance is widely available. Counselling or therapy can be very effective but be careful about who you choose – if you can, go with someone who is personally recommended. I found that 80% of the value was in the first session, but none of the subsequent sessions had the same power. Many alternative therapists of different sorts seek to create dependence rather than independence, so be careful to judge how long you want to continue for.

It is very important to distinguish between functional and dysfunctional natural languages. We are the product of evolution. It has taken literally millions of years to evolve to our current state. By definition we are the product of generations of ancestors who were good at propagating their genes. Our ancestors discovered that the way to be genetically successful was to live in tribes and to collaborate for both individual, tribal and species success. Functional behaviours might be described as those that promote the overall long-term success and well-being of our genes, those of our tribe and those of our species. Native American Indians defined their long-term responsibility as being seven generations. In contrast dysfunctional behaviours are those which focus on the narrow and short term to the detriment of broader and longer term considerations, including those of the next seven generations.

One of the questions that people often ask is; 'yes, but what if someone is authentically a paedophile (or whatever)?' I believe that these pathological behaviours are simply more extreme forms of dysfunctionality generated through more extreme lifetime and childhood traumas. Underneath it all there is a functional person who is screaming to get out, though they may never be able to.

The other question this raises in our still prudish society is that of homosexuality and how that can be in the long-term interest of our gene pool and therefore functional. I don't know. What I do know is that homosexuality is entirely natural and is consistent with what happens in every other species. In our society homosexuals have one significant advantage over others – they have already had to go through the process of 'coming out' and, perhaps as a consequence, are often more in touch with who they are.

I believe that every one of us has a natural language within which we are uniquely brilliant. By living in that language you will be able to enjoy an easy success in whatever you choose to do. The next challenge is that not every natural language is highly valued in our society. We will address the question of how to make a living by being yourself later in Section III.

PREPARATION 4: WHAT IS MY POINT IN LIFE?

Native American Indians believe that everyone (and everything) has a special and unique purpose in life.

What a great idea.

I like to call this our 'point', after all if we do not have a point to our lives then we are pointless and that would be very disappointing. In our society the forces of conformity and distraction conspire to disguise our point from us almost entirely. Many of us live our entire lives without ever working out why we are here, while others stumble across their point almost by accident.

Every day I hear stories about how people have found a new meaning in life, how they have shrugged off the shackles of their old life to dedicate themselves to their purpose. Often this discovery seems to be made through crisis, but I do not think that crisis is necessarily required. I believe that crisis is only a catalyst for people to take stock of their lives and begin to think more deeply about who they are and what they are doing. The crisis shakes them out of their passivity rather than actually being the cause of change.

How can you start the process of identifying your true purpose without waiting for a crisis?

Perhaps through the previous two steps you have been able to identify your natural language and your beliefs. If you have you are well on the way to identifying your purpose.

Natural languages and beliefs are assets, tools that you can direct in any way that you please. However, once you find it – your point – it will be easy to recognize since it will not be an option for you whether you pursue it or not. Your point will make such sense to you, be so easy for you to apply yourself to and be so natural for you to do that you will seriously wonder why you wasted all of those years doing anything else.

Your point has a gravitational pull for you. Once you stop fighting it and learn to trust yourself far from having to find your point you will not be able to stop if from finding you. In fact, it might be so obvious to you that initially you mistake it for something quite mundane. It may even be quite an anticlimax when you find it, but once you engage with it you will not be able to return to carrying out someone else's dysfunctional purpose.

The challenge here is that we are not generally conditioned to wait for things to happen. We are conditioned to search, strive, try and, above all, to be busy. It seems counter-intuitive that the search for our deepest meaning should involve sitting around and doing nothing. Our society likes us to do stuff and to buy stuff if we want to achieve anything. When dieting for example it is not enough to simply eat less and go for a walk. Our society has created several industries around dieting; diet food, diet exercise, diet clubs, diet publishing and so on.

Soul searching is about introspection and quiet contemplation, avoiding distraction and existing as a human being for a while rather than human doing. It is interesting that many of our wisest leaders such as Nelson Mandela, Aung San Suu Kyi, Vaclav Havel and Mahatma Gandhi have spent time in prison where they have had time for contemplation without distraction to develop their thinking and identity. We also need to remember that the power of figuring out your natural language and your point during contemplation can go the wrong way if it is founded on a dysfunctional world view; Hitler also spent time in prison. The force, as Obi Wan might say, does truly have a dark side.

I remember a constant impression of white noise in my life; I remember feeling that it would be really nice to be in prison or hospital for a bit, just to get the chance to figure things out. I've never been to prison although I did spend a week in hospital. As I mentioned earlier, I create my space on my bike. When I started cycling I found that I could not go as fast or as far as I thought I should. I identified my nutrition as a limiting factor and set about learning more about food and diet. Once I had made the necessary changes to my diet and eating habits I still found myself more limited than I felt I should be, and identified my mind as the limiting factor. I then went on a journey of understanding enough of my own psychology to successfully remove that limit.

In the course of a few years I went from being slightly overweight and heading for a fairly predictable 21st century lifestyle – of overeating, over drinking and being overweight – to cycling 700km over the Pyrenees in four and a half days.

There is no shortcut to identifying your point in life. However, there are a few questions that you might like to ponder on what might help you to find and articulate it.

1   What is your natural language?

It seems counter-intuitive that the search for our deepest meaning should involve sitting around and doing nothing

2   Who do you want to do it for?

3   What is the outcome for them?

4   How are you going to do it?

5   Why?

Take your time. This is a big question and you will need to work hard at it. Give yourself permission to take the time to figure out the answer, this is a big chunk of your life we are talking about and it is well worth getting it right.

Making your point happen will be far, far harder if not impossible without good health. However you interpret it, success means very little if achieving it makes you sick. The following 'Actions' offer no guarantees that you will never get sick, but they tell the story of my journey to caring about my health, which facilitates my work today.

ACTION 1: EATING YOUR ENERGY

If you are going to do anything amazing you will need strength and endurance, a strong platform from which to do it. To do this you will need to make the most of your mind and body by feeding yourself with good fuels and preparing yourself with good exercise.

The saying goes 'You are what you eat' and it is true in a very literal sense. Only 2% of the atoms in your body are more than one year old. Every year our bodies are 98% rebuilt, cell by cell. This process is managed and regulated, by us, with mind-boggling dexterity without even noticing.

Clever filtration processes evaluate whatever you ingest, whenever you eat, drink and breathe. The bad stuff is expelled and the good stuff is sorted into fuel and building blocks. The fuel is used to power us through our chosen activities and the building blocks are used for building and maintenance.

Who manages all of this? You do. Somewhere in your mind there is active control of all of the wonderful systems that keep all of these systems functioning. So, as Deepak Chopra says in *Perfect Health*, the process of aging or getting sick is fundamentally a process of forgetting how to put ourselves back together again properly.

However, this miraculous subconscious system relies entirely on what our conscious mind chooses to put into the system in the first place. We can really help our building and maintenance system to do its job well by ensuring that what we put in is the best stuff for the job.

In my simplification of this massively complex process, fuels are things like oxygen, water, sugars and fats, in descending order of volume. Building blocks are the important minerals and proteins that should be in our food and drink.

A complete guide to nutrition is beyond the scope of this book. The intention of this section is to spark your interest and encourage you to take more care over what you buy and eat. There are plenty of good nutrition resources on the market. If you are serious and especially if you are taking up exercise, I recommend *Optimum Sports Nutrition* by Michael Colgan.

Here are the fuels in descending order.

Oxygen

If it was only available bottled, marketed and sold I am sure that we would take a great deal more care of our oxygen than we do. The quality of the air that we breathe is crucial to our health. Sadly most of us, including those living in the countryside, breathe very poor quality air. It is not easy to do anything about this but it is certainly worth bearing in mind when you choose where to live and when thinking about how much time to spend in or near heavy traffic.

You are not entirely subject to where you live, although Colgan says 'You cannot hope to be a serious athlete and live in a polluted city!' One easy step you can take is to practice breathing more deeply and actually using the full extent of your lungs.

Clients find it highly embarrassing when I require workshop groups to start the session by standing up and doing a couple of minutes of really deep breathing. But it has a serious point. Try it now. Stand up and really fill your lungs deeply and breathe. Can you feel the blood rushing to your head? Do you get a little buzz as if you had just had a really strong shot of coffee? That is your brain and body being properly oxygenated.

Any time you are feeling a little tired and lethargic or are about to embark on something complex or challenging, straighten your body as much as you can and breathe deeply. Give yourself the best instant hit you can and feel the power.

Water

This is the easy one. Drink loads. Because you need to drink so much of it, ideally your water should be clean – not just filtered but actually distilled. You can buy home distillers, which sit under the kitchen sink and give you plenty of really clean water. However, this may be taking things a little far for most people, including me.

If your lips, hands or the skin around your eyes are ever dry it may mean you are badly dehydrated. It takes several days of drinking too little for these symptoms to show, so if you have them regularly you may be chronically dehydrated.

The amount you need to drink is affected by circumstances:

- *The amount of exercise you do*. Heavy exercise requires about a litre per hour plus a litre in the hour before and another litre within the hour after you finish.

- *Humidity*. Humidity is a greater influence than heat. Air-conditioning also extracts moisture from the air, so if your workplace is air-conditioned you will need to drink more. In the tropics, where humidity is high, dehydration is much less of a problem than in a desert area at the same temperature.

- *The amount you drink*. When you drink too little your body adapts to some extent to cope with being dehydrated. The cost of this coping is that your body will constantly underperform. When you drink enough your body uses more water to make things work better. So one of the things you will notice as you drink more is that you need to drink even more.

As with most things there is a great deal of advice about how much water to drink and it is often contradictory. The best understanding that I can divine is that we need about one and a half litres per day as an absolute functional minimum – depending on body size. At this level your body is on the edge of compromising on performance, especially if you actually do anything physical. I weigh around 80kgs and on a normal day without exercise I will drink three litres of water.

It is important to note that we are talking about water here and not beer, tea or coffee. Nothing, except possibly some isotonic sports drinks, hydrates the way that water does, and many of our favourite drinks actually dehydrate us by being diuretics and making the water pass through faster. So the three litres is in addition to diuretics such as tea coffee or beer.

The other important element is timing. If you drink your three litres of water all in one go your system will be flooded and you will pee most of it out. Your body can only absorb about one litre per hour so more than that is pointless. And if you add anything to the water like sugar or juice it is likely to slow that absorption down.

And I said water was the simple one …

Sugars

Strictly speaking, sugars are simple carbohydrates that only give very short busts of energy and play havoc with our insulin system by constantly engaging it to manage the sugar spikes in our modern diet. In fact our modern diet, high in simple sugars is responsible for the huge growth in the incidence of diabetes. So actually simple sugars/carbohydrates are not really what you want at all.

What you really want are complex carbohydrates like rice, cereals, potatoes, fruits and vegetables, pasta and bread. These give you energy and are the primary fuel for regular activity, and especially for endurance exercise. Your reserves will usually see you through one to two hours of exercise at which point, if you have not taken some more on board, you will hit what runners call 'the wall'.

'The wall' is also something you can experience in a busy day at the office, and many people who routinely skip breakfast find themselves lethargic after lunch, because their body is prioritizing digesting lunch because it urgently needs some fuel.

Breakfast is the most important meal of the day from an energy point of view. Make sure you have a good one of fruit, cereals and bread to power you through your day. From an energy point of view it is generally better to top up with snacks (fruit, not biscuits!) and have smaller meals so that your blood sugar never dips.

Complex carbohydrates should make up about a third of your diet, or more if you are doing endurance exercises like running, cycling, swimming or walking and the less modified or tampered with they are the better. Processed foods and refined wheat lose their energy and minerals and can play havoc with the stomach. Wheat allergy is incredibly common these days. What people usually mean by wheat allergy is intolerance to refined wheat and, often, the symptoms are the feeling of being bloated, and flatulence. So wherever possible go for the unrefined, whole-grain breads, wholewheat pasta, brown rice and so on.

Fats

We need fats in our diet; what we do not need are saturated fats. Saturated fats are the bad fats found in dairy products, meats and fried food. Good fats are found in extra virgin olive oil and fish.

I have lived for years without buying butter or margarine. Try spreading your jam or whatever directly onto your toast – you will be surprised at how little you miss the butter. Use extra virgin olive oil in your cooking – the 'extra' means it is unprocessed.

For meat, stick to low fat options such as chicken and turkey. Game can also be a good alternative – things like venison and rabbit. Pork, beef and lamb are all much higher in fat, unless you go for the very highest quality, lowest fat, lean cuts or mince.

Learn to read food labels. If you want to have less that 20% of your body made up of fat you should aim for a diet which is less that 20% fat BY CALORIFIC INTAKE. In the UK and most other places fat is labelled as a percentage of weight – not of calories.

For example a soup might be only 1.2 grams of fat per 100grams – only 1.2% fat you think? Wrong. As a rule of thumb you should multiply the fat content by ten and then calculate as a percentage of the energy in calories (usually labelled kcal). In our soup example, 1.2 grams of fat multiplies into 12 calories of fat and as a percentage of the total of 57 kcal, that is more like 21% – not bad, but not as good as you thought.

20% body fat is a good target for men but is too low for women. Women have a higher percentage of body fat than men and 20% would be seriously low for a woman where 22–25% is more suitable.

Building blocks

Minerals and proteins are the building blocks. You need to have minerals and proteins to maintain the annual atom replacement programme. Without them, the programme is compromised and you age and get sick.

Good sources of protein are meat, fish, nuts, pulses and eggs – but remember to balance the fat when choosing meat. The best way to get your minerals in is through fruit and vegetables with as little preparation or processing as possible. The more fruit and vegetables are cooked or peeled, the more of the vital goodness is lost.

Not all fruit and vegetables (or fish or meat) are equal

Minerals in plants are absorbed in the microscopic quantities that we need from the soil. It takes about three years for crops to deplete soil of minerals if the same or similar crops are grown on the same land.

I remember when I was brought up in Suffolk, in a wonderful place surrounded by fields. At school I was taught about crop rotation and fields laying fallow every third year. I thought this was a great idea, because I would be able to go and play in the cropless fields. I waited and waited. It seems that in the breadbasket of England, education had yet to catch up with intensive agriculture.

When chemical farming was popularized just after World War II it seemed like a miracle. It was found that if you poured nitrogen and phosphates onto the soil you could dramatically increase yields and get rid of that unprofitable fallow year. The crops looked great, bigger than ever, it was truly a miracle. In addition, the chemical companies had found someone to buy all of those chemicals that they had just lost their biggest client for – the armaments factories. Since then many more chemicals have been developed for farming.

The problem is that after three years or so the minerals in the soil are still gone and the only minerals going into the crops are the ones in the fertilizers. The only way to get all of that good stuff back into the food is to care for the soil properly taking the time to plough in manure, rotating with different crops each year and letting the soil rest every third year.

The only commercial food that you can be confident is grown using these methods today is organic food. Which is why if you want to do the best for your health you have to choose to eat organic wherever possible. It is worth noting that the Soil Association believes that it takes two years for the soil to recover from the damage done by intensive farming, which is why it takes so long to gain organic certification.

For meat and fish the arguments are, if anything, stronger. An intensively farmed chicken puts on 2 kilos of weight on only 2.5 kilos of feed in its pathetic 42-day life. Chickens, other livestock and farmed fish are routinely injected or fed with antibiotics – not to keep them healthy but because it makes them grow faster. In the 1950s a farmer in the US, who was feeding his chicks on a waste material from the production of an antibiotic called aureomycin thinking it might offer disease prevention benefits, noticed that the chicks were growing far faster than normal. The use of antibiotics as growth promoters rapidly created a new industry and spread around the world of intensive agriculture.

All of this is supposedly to make food cheaper, but of course the massive cost of BSE, foot-and-mouth, salmonella, e-coli etc. are not reflected in supermarket prices. We still pay the costs, indirectly, through our taxes. If these costs (plus the costs of cleaning up polluted rivers and the healthcare costs) were internalized to intensive farming it would be massively more expensive than organic. Unfortunately they are not. So organic foods still appear to be more expensive.

Cost and availability are still issues for organic food in many areas. However, your health, and that of your family, must be one of your absolute baseline priorities. And for most people reading this book it is not a choice between food or shelter. It is a choice to buy slightly more expensive food or that CD/pint of beer/pack of cigarettes/cinema ticket. My recommendation is stay healthy, have more energy and spend the extra on buying organic.

If any of those reports that say 'traditionally' (how can they use that word when referring to intensive, industrialized agriculture) farmed food is just as good for you as organic food, just remember to ask – who is paying for the research? Ten-to-one it is one of the vested interests. As John Humphrys says in his book *The Great Food Gamble*, 'The Thoughtful Sceptics say there is not enough evidence (that organic food is better for you). They have a point; much more research needs to be done. But there is a powerful lobby opposed to organic farming who have no interest in evidence or research (which shows that organic food is better for you). That lobby includes the vested interests: the agrochemical companies who sell the pesticides and synthetic fertilizers, the biotech companies who want to sell their genetically modified seeds; the Barley Barons who have made small fortunes from farming subsidies; the politicians who are afraid to admit they have got it wrong over the years and are afraid to upset the big vested interests.'

Supplements

Most nutritionists say that for the average person a balanced diet is all that is required and that supplements are not necessary. However, if you have got this far I hope that you have absolutely no ambition to be average. I hope that your ambition is to be extraordinary and exceptional. I believe that a few supplements can help you achieve this.

When you are buying mineral supplements it is worth bearing in mind that these are building blocks and, as such, it will take six months of regular consumption for them to be fully effective. After some experimentation I have come to what I believe is a good compromise.

Each day we take:

- 1 gram Vitamin C (for the immune system, take up to 4 grams when you have a cold);

- 1 multi-vitamin and mineral supplement;

- 1 gram fish oil; and

- 500mg glucosamine (for joints, especially if you are exercising a lot).

It is also worth bearing in mind that it is not possible to patent vitamins or minerals. The pharmaceutical companies hate the way that they are sold as health products but do not have to go through the same stringent testing as their chemicals. It is also worth bearing in mind that the pharmaceutical companies fund many of the nutritionists – either directly or via research grants – who are put in front of the media to say that supplements are unnecessary.

All of this might lead you to question why the EU are so keen to change the laws on the sale of vitamins and minerals and drastically reduce the quantities in which they can be sold. According to British MEP Lord Stockton in a letter to Prime Minister Tony Blair 'This directive has nothing to do with safety and everything to do with the commercial benefits to a few big European pharmaceutical companies.'

You will notice the benefits of good fuelling right away, you'll have more energy, a greater ability to deal with situations and, after six months of taking good building blocks, you will know that your body is ready to take on more, and is more reliable when you push it hard.

However, vital as it is, physical fuel and exercise is not enough. We need to nourish and exercise both our mind and our body.

ACTION 2: EXERCISE YOUR MIND

Finding and living in your natural language and knowing and living your point in life is fresh, organic breakfast, lunch and dinner to your mind and soul. The energy you recover by simply being yourself rather than pouring energy into maintaining an ego is startling and that energy can be used to multiply itself and give you even more.

In our evolutionary upbringing for three million years we developed to be highly active. Our bodies have developed highly sophisticated systems for turning our fuels into three basic energy systems for different levels of activity.

You might characterize them as stroll, steady and scramble.

When we are in stroll mode our body is working at a very low level and can use its most efficient slow burning fuel – fat. Fat is used to fuel us while we walk or sit around the TV/camp fire. In our evolutionary upbringing fat was highly prized by our bodies as it is the fuel that will keep you going if there are long gaps between successful hunts. It is no coincidence that high fat foods, such as chocolate, are the ones we crave when we are feeling low.

Finding and living in your natural language and knowing and living your point in life is fresh, organic breakfast, lunch and dinner to your mind and soul.

When we are in steady mode such as running, cycling or swimming, the energy source shifts progressively towards using sugars and carbohydrates. The sugars are stored in our blood and kidneys and combine with an increasing amount of oxygen – breathing becomes heavier as exercise intensity increases, which is why it is known as aerobic exercise. This energy source can be used for one to two hours, depending on intensity, before it is exhausted, when you 'hit the wall'.

In scramble mode we need our muscles to access fuel fast, and our stored fat and sugars cannot get there quickly enough. This is for very short bursts of extreme effort lasting only a few seconds. Here, we use energy stored in our muscles and do not even need oxygen to use it, which is why it is known as anaerobic exercise. When you lift something heavy you will often hold your breath as you do it and catch up on the breathing later. Working at this level is extremely stressful for your body. Before you can do this with any regularity you need to be very fit and to include significant recovery afterwards.

In modern life there is less call for sprinting after prey or away from predators or even for long walks in search of food or water. Much of modern life is led with our minds at full stretch and our bodies passive. This is not how we have evolved to be. When our bodies are passive for any length of time they tend to go into decline. Our ability to use our fuels, muscles and organs diminishes. To keep ourselves at optimum performance it is vital that we exercise several times a week and stay fit.

Ideally this exercise should be in the steady mode probably taking the form of fast walking, running, cycling or swimming, some sport or gym activity. Doing something largely on your own has the advantage that you can combine it with your introspection, but it can require a higher level of motivation to keep it going.

If you are not fit it can take a great deal of motivation and persistence to get fit in the first place. Once you have got fit you will be very reluctant to let it slip and have to start again from scratch.

When I talk to people about regular exercise they often say that I must be very lucky to have the time to exercise, implying that if they had the time, they would. This is nonsense. Like so many other decisions in life it is about priorities. If you make exercise a priority you will make time for it. I spent seven years using commuting time as exercise time, going from one side of London to the other by bike. At its most extreme I did Twickenham to Orpington (21 miles each way) for three months.

Today, although I no longer live in London, I use a folding bike on my weekly visits there to make sure I do not waste the opportunity for exercise. I also save money by avoiding tubes and taxis and now with the advent of congestion charging, Londoners have no excuse at all not to get out on their bikes. Although it does still take some practice to get used to the traffic and find the best routes.

How many journeys do you make that could be done on foot or by bike? How much time do you spend sitting in front of TV or in the pub which could be spent exercising? How much ineffective time do you spend at work which could be spent getting fitter so that you would have more energy to do your work better? If you prioritize exercise you will make time for it. If you do not feel that you can make those choices then you need to ask 'who is in control of your life?'

ACTION 3: TAKING CONTROL OF YOUR LIFE

As we have discovered, much in our upbringing and our societal conditioning is about encouraging us to conform and to be lead rather than to lead our own lives. In the 'Age of Empire' it suited the leaders of the country of industry and of the military to educate the masses to be followers and not leaders. The elite would be educated to be leaders and thus the class system would be maintained.

As *The Hitch-Hikers Guide to the Galaxy* says on the subject, 'In these enlightened days, of course, no one believes a word of it.'

Finding your natural language, learning to be honest with yourself, understanding the difference between perception and reality, identifying your point, eating your energy and exercising your mind are all steps along a journey of discovery and they are preparation for making the change.

The change is when you decide to 'come out' for yourself, and only be who you really are in all circumstances and situations. In practice, the change will probably take the form of a growing confidence over a period of weeks or months, but at some point you will realize that you have the confidence to be yourself in more and more situations, and that the time is coming to close off the situations in which you still feel uncomfortable being yourself.

It is time to come out as yourself.

ACTION 4: AVOIDING DISTRACTION AND INSPIRING CHANGE

A great deal of the mass media consumed today seems like distraction at best; at worst, some kind of remotely administered mass anaesthetic. The concept of weapons of mass distraction first occurred to me on a truly awful charter flight. Throughout the flight the cabin crew kept the passengers largely distracted by constant messages, entertainment, food and drink; anything to keep us from complaining.

Having identified this phenomenon once I began to realize that it is in fact all around me. TV entertainment (particularly soap operas), newspapers, fashion, magazines, restaurants, many films, sport and so on. All of these can be distractions designed to keep us from thinking too deeply and asking too many difficult questions, challenging our leaders, or actually doing anything to change the situation.

Your tolerance to distraction and your ability to identify inspiration will change as you travel this journey. To start with, inspiration will be harder to find and most things will be distractions. As you learn and begin to become more aware so inspiration will start to leap out at you from quite unlikely places.

We pay more to be distracted than we do to anyone except the government and the bank. Compare the amount we pay sports and pop stars with the amount that we pay to educators or healthcare workers, for example.

In *The Matrix*, Neo feels that the world is not quite as it seems and spends his time searching cyberspace for answers. His search leads him to Morpheus who shows him that the world he experiences is, in fact, a computer generated dreamworld designed to distract humanities minds while the computers milk their bodies for energy. An analogy for our times, perhaps?

Once you start to look at distraction a bit more carefully you realize that it is actually far more highly valued in our society than almost anything else. We pay more to be distracted than we do to anyone except the government and the bank. Compare the amount we pay sports and pop stars with the amount that we pay to educators or healthcare workers, for example.

The government are tremendous distracters in their own right and will often use distraction as a way of diverting attention from things they would prefer that we did not notice. Whenever a 'scandal' is clogging up media time you can bet that something more interesting is going virtually unreported.

The alternative to distraction is inspiration, and although some distraction is perfectly justifiable I suggest that there is often a good deal of opportunity to introduce more inspiration into our lives and reduce the amount of distraction.

There is plenty of inspiration in films and books and if you are selective there is also a surprising amount of inspiration on TV, radio and even in newspapers. It is just a question of being conscious of the difference. In order to facilitate your journey, consume as much inspiration as you can get your hands on and avoid distraction.

I love to find wisdom in movies, even some quite unlikely ones. Good examples are:

- *Dead Poets Society* is about freedom of thought.

- *Shawshank Redemption* is about persistence in the face of the establishment when you know you are right.

- *Groundhog Day* is about the way life throws lessons at us.

- *The Matrix* is about the nature of the system and about our unlimited potential if we choose it.

- *Fight Club* (if you are feeling brave) is a harsh wake-up call and reality check with a great deal of wisdom.

Books that have inspired me include:

- *Ishmael, My Ishmael* and *The Story of B* by Daniel Quinn. Reading *Ishmael* really encouraged me to look at the world differently and to keep asking questions.

- *The Alchemist* by Paul Coelho reminded me that I already have what I am searching for and the best place to start looking is inside.

- *And We Are Doing It* by JT Ross Jackson helped me to understand the nature of the system and that there are alternatives.

- *The Hitch Hikers Guide to the Galaxy* by Douglas Adams covers just about everything.

- *Perfect Health* by Deepak Chopra helped me to understand that my health is my responsibility and my problem.

- *Optimum Sports Nutrition* by Dr Michael Colgan includes all of the nutrition education I should have had at school.

- *The Invitation* by Oriah Mountain Dreamer – check with yourself and see how you are doing.

- *Jonathan Livingston Seagull* by Richard Bach reveals the nature of conformity and the battle for individuality.

Once you start to focus on it you will be able to find wisdom and inspiration almost everywhere. Even on trashy TV and the in the news.

Finding inspiration is the search for new ideas. In spite of appearances there is no one right way to do anything. There are always options and alternatives (including not doing it at all). When you are looking for inspiration you are looking for alternatives to the current way that you do things, like make a living. Finding alternatives that work for you will mean that you no longer have to do things that create a tension for you.

Taking conscious control of the media you consume is an important step. Whilst you are anaesthetized by the distraction and accepting the solutions offered by the media you will find it difficult to come up with your own solutions.

ACTION 5: EDITING YOUR ADDRESS BOOK

We pick up friends as we pass through life, at school, in jobs and so on. Very often we maintain friendships out of habit and out of a need to be liked that stems from our lack of self-confidence. However, our friendships can become limiting and hold us back.

When I was facing up to changing my life I made absolutely certain that the only person I discussed it with would support and contribute to my thinking. I did not mention it to anyone else until it was a *fait accompli*. Afterwards it became clear who my friends were. Although it can be a bit scary to edit your address book if your friends do not support you in being yourself, you may want to ask yourself if they are really your friends.

Taking conscious control of your friendships, especially during your time of change, ensures that you minimize the confusion of conflicting messages and that you spend your time and energy moving towards your point rather than being deflected from it.

ACTION 6: CHANGING HABITS

If you have spent years not truly being yourself, starting to be yourself will involve changing your behaviour. I often think that there is a difference between doing and being, for example the difference between dieting and losing weight. Dieting is a process of reading books or magazines and being fussy about what you eat. Losing weight is about eating less and doing more exercise.

In every situation you have a choice. It may not always seem like it but you are in control of your life and you are the one who chooses to do this or compromise on that. The first step to change is to understand that you are already making choices, even if those choices are not always conscious.

By bringing all of those decisions up to a conscious level and challenging yourself as to why you do, or do not do, certain things you can begin to understand yourself and the decisions you take and to start making conscious choices.

Whenever you are facing a decision your answer will be within you. Knowing your point and your natural language gives you some easy criteria:

- Will this help me to realize my point?

- Is this within the scope of my natural language?

If it passes this rational test you can then listen to your intuition and interpret your feelings and the clues that are around you. You should find that the business of making balanced decisions becomes easier.

With good balanced decision making comes the opportunity to change things in your life. Most of us will make resolutions that we fail to keep at some point or another. There are a number of reasons for this failure: it was not the right resolution, or time, or you set yourself a target that you knew you were unlikely to achieve to reinforce your self image of inadequacy, or it was down to simple peer pressure.

Do not beat yourself up for failing to stick to resolutions, it is all part of the searching process as you search for things that you can stick to. It is far better to keep trying new resolutions than to give up and stop making the effort. As long as you keep at it you will, at some point, start to find that you can do what you commit to.

When you make resolutions using balanced decision making you are far more likely to stick to them because they are taken wholeheartedly and with a meaning and place in your life. This means that you can make real change happen.

It can even be good to make changes just to test this theory, to prove that you can and build confidence. Try giving something up – coffee, TV, whatever. This is good preparation for making real changes as part of a coherent plan, rather than in isolation.

ACTION 7: MAKING YOUR PLAN

'If you don't design your own life plan, chances are you'll fall into someone else's plan. And guess what they have planned for you? Not much.'

Jim Rohn

Frequently when I talk about life planning with people their initial reaction is that planning your life is rather cynical and precludes the possibility of serendipity.

My response is that the difference between planning and not planning is like the difference between going for a walk and going on a journey. When you go for a walk you can enjoy your surroundings and be guided by the path but it is no good if you actually want to get somewhere specific. If you want to get somewhere in your life it is like a journey. You will need to understand your starting situation and your destination and need to identify the critical points in between. Although a life may contain many walks, over-all it should be a journey and not just a series of walks.

Enjoying yourself involves being where you want to be, with the people you want to be with, doing what you want to be doing as much of the time as possible. I do not believe that this can be achieved without planning.

The other response to planning is more worrying. Many people I have spoken to about this see planning in the context of mortality. They see planning as futile because we cannot predict when we will die. They believe that rather than wasting energy and emotion planning we should simply enjoy the time that we have now and not worry about tomorrow until we are there.

I believe that this is not only a fundamental misconception but it is also potentially self-fulfilling. With no purpose and no plan, what would be the point in having a long and healthy life?

Enjoying yourself involves being where you want to be, with the people you want to be with, doing what you want to be doing as much of the time as possible. I do not believe that this can be achieved without planning.

In any case planning is very simple.

1   Know where you are.

2   Know your destination (at least roughly).

3   Plan the general route.

4   Plan the initial part of the route in detail.

In the course of reading this book I hope you have started to understand your current situation and that you have been able to identify your ultimate destination – your point.

Now it is time to get the hang of planning and work out how you are going to achieve your point. One of the other concerns that people raise about planning is to ask what happens when something occurs that invalidates the plan? Easy. You modify the plan to take account of the changed circumstances, or you make a new one.

Start by writing your starting situation and your destination down on Post-it notes and stick them on a large empty wall, with a significant gap between them, where you can see them every day. Put the beginning on the left and the end on the right. Think of the gap between the two as time and divide it by the number of months or years over which your plan lasts.

Identify some of the critical points between the two. Write them on more Post-its and stick them up on the wall in between the beginning and end and try to put them into a sensible order with a reasonable time gap between them.

Now go to the first gap between the start and the first critical point and do the same again. Fill in the gap with actions and critical points. Keep playing with this, moving the notes around, putting new ones up and taking others down, over hours, days or months, as long as you feel you need to (or can bear having your wall covered in sticky paper). Once you feel it looks like a plan take the notes down in order and put them somewhere you can refer to. I like to copy each note to a PowerPoint slide so that I can still see them in order, add new ones easily, or delete them or move them around. If you prefer not to use a computer you could achieve the same effect by writing each one on a sheet of A4 and putting them into a ring binder.

Play with the medium. Use different coloured notes to identify targets or dependencies (things that have to be done before you can do the next thing). Use different coloured pens to denote conditions that will have to be achieved or ideas and so on. You can also identify dependencies and dependents (things that cannot be done until after a particular action has been completed) by writing them in the top left and right corners respectively so that for each given action you know what needs to be done before and after it.

I find that once I have made a plan I rarely need to refer to it. I keep the critical points in my mind and generally do them or adapt them. Others prefer to track their plan diligently, entering dates when they achieve goals or keeping it up to date to reflect changes that occur. Do whatever works for you. In the first place, the important thing is to have a destination and a plan for how to get there. The next most important thing is to act on it.

ACTION 8: COMING OUT AND BEING YOURSELF

At some point on this journey you will come to a point where the cohesion that holds your old life together is no longer strong enough to hold back your energy. When you reach this point you will have to consider how you are going to tell the world.

To me, telling the world felt like a huge challenge to overcome.

In reality, it was a bit of an anticlimax.

The world did not end; there was no huge earthquake. Everything continued pretty much as before except that I knew with a quiet confidence that I would never, ever feel the need compromise my soul for anyone.

As I wrote in the Preface, the way I told the world was in an e-mail to 4000 people, many of whom I did not know. I don't think it is necessary to be that public, although I will be very happy to publish your story on the Authentic Business Web site – www.authenticbusiness.co.uk.

However I do think it is important to make some sort of public commitment to say this is who I am and this is what I stand for.

There will be those who criticize you. This is their problem, not yours. I received criticism from both friends and some of the 4000 people I had written to. I realized that those people are totally entitled to their opinion but it did not need to have any effect on me because for each one who did criticize there were twenty who offered total support.

I quickly learned not to take criticism personally and realized that generally their views were born out of their own fears, insecurities and regrets. I realized that when people criticize it is usually as a result of something that they identify, consciously or subconsciously, in themselves, rather than a problem that they have with you or what you are doing.

The reason it is important to make the public statement is that once it is out there, you no longer need to feel apologetic about who you are. You can be proud. Proud of who you are and what you are good at. Proud of your past, your future and your now. You can state, with openness and pride, what you are good at and what you are not good at. You no longer need to compare yourself to others, or wonder or worry about what people think of you.

You are you. Proud. Unique. Brilliant.

> 'This is not the end. This is not the beginning of the end. This is the end of the beginning.'

> *Winston Churchill*

Being the Change

3

For authenticity to work it has to work everywhere and at every level. It has to work in relationships, it has to work for income, it has to work for parenting.

This book is called *Authentic: How to Make a Living by Being Yourself* because it is about being authentic and how to turn that into a living that supports you and your own and brings you all that you need.

This section is about life after the change has been made. There is no point in making the change if it does not reward you with greater happiness, satisfaction and success in every area of your life. This section describes how being yourself is all you need to be and that if you do it, really do it, you will find that the world starts to work with you most of the time. You become lucky.

For me, life has never been easier or more rewarding. After years of confusion and struggle I am largely clear about what I am doing and challenges are enjoyed.

In this section we will look at:

- Getting started

- Working for yourself

- Validating the plan

- Simplify, simplify

- Time and motion

- Finding collaborators

- Designing your organization

- Competition

- The meaning of success

GETTING STARTED

I left my job to start Authentic Business. My partner (now wife) had no job either. We had moved to a new city six weeks earlier. We were in a rented flat. We had a little money to last us a few months.

I was sustained by the certainty that if I did the right thing I would have all that I needed. 11 months later we bought our dream home. I am running my own business, doing something I really enjoy and I rarely feel overworked, stressed or under pressure. We have all that we need.

The only reason for saying this is to demonstrate that it can be done.

I do not want this to sound smug or as though it was easy – either to make the commitment or to go and do it. The journey was not without incident. We ran close to the edge and we came close to running out of money, even though we had pared back our spending. There were times when I was challenged and tested by people and friends. My confidence never wavered. I knew all along that if I did the right thing, it would work out.

That faith was bolstered by the huge support I had from the people I told my story to and the curious way that the world seemed to conspire to support me and guide me.

I wrote a detailed business plan for Authentic Business, more perhaps out of habit than a need for understanding. The plan was conventional in the sense that it was about a business designed to make money. Since then I have come to understand that the core philosophy of the business resonates widely but the ideas I had for making money were optimistic and I had failed to properly value my own ideas and work. Here I am, even at this stage, still lacking the self-confidence to value myself properly.

I am running my own business, doing something I really enjoy and I rarely feel overworked, stressed or under pressure. We have all that we need.

Four months later, with a shiny new Web site, a database of 4000 people recommended by friends as being likely to be interested, and a selection of inspiring articles, I launched Authentic Business as an on-line newsletter. The response I had to that launch can be seen in the Preface. It was wonderful. I spent the next three months writing articles, e-mailing people who responded to the newsletter, meeting many of the people who got in touch, reading articles and publishing them.

Three months after launch I was starting to pick up my first contract work and doing client work alongside running the newsletter.

WORKING FOR YOURSELF

Working with clients in the corporate sector, I am frequently astonished at just how willingly and completely many ordinary employees are consumed with making profits for their company. Although I have done it myself in the past, I now find it hard to comprehend how these people appear to be so willing to commit such a high proportion of their time and energy to making someone else rich.

Quoted corporations are not generally designed to make their workers rich or successful in any meaningful dimension. And only a tiny percentage of private companies are able to offer success to a tiny proportion of their staff. Big companies will trade your loyalty, hard work, energy and time for money and precious little else.

As a concept, Authentic Business is about making you and those close to you the primary beneficiaries of your brilliance and energy, and our cohabitants (all other living things) on this planet the secondary beneficiaries. Authentic Business is about having all that you need. The clever bit is knowing what you need and not expending your energy to get anything else.

You may want to work for yourself or to work for a company that shares your point and worldview. That does not mean, if you have a job, that you should spend your time desperate to leave. You can see your job as a practical expedient to get you to where you want to be in terms of learning, experience, contacts and a savings safety net by making it a time-limited part of your plan to regain your freedom. Making that plan and that shift is set out below in 'Validating the plan'.

VALIDATING THE PLAN

The plan I wrote for Authentic Business was written for a prospective investor. In the event I realized that imagining I needed an investor and spending time looking for one was taking up time, which was eating into cash reserves. I might just as well get on with it. I was also deeply suspicious of the idea of giving away any control or influence over the business.

As it turned out, the plan was most useful for clarifying my own thinking so I could actually write it down coherently and then, using that coherence of thought, to explain the ideas to others. Although I did actually give a copy to my bank manager, I am not sure that any one, apart from me, has ever actually read it.

If you have worked with the Post-it notes as described in 'Action 7: Making the plan' you will now have a basic plan and chronology for your life. If you want to turn this into an income and a way of life you may want to write it out as a detailed business plan. As suggested above, writing it out will surface issues in your logic and thinking that you will have to resolve.

Perhaps more useful and certainly simpler than the normal business plan is the five-year plan. While the business plan is useful as a clarifying and focusing process it is unlikely that you or anyone else will refer to it again except out of nostalgic interest in a few years time.

The five-year plan is simple and should provide a real point of reference for you and anyone else you work with. Each year is given a title, which is to be the theme for that year. Year five or the last year if you think it needs to be longer (or shorter) should embody your overall vision.

For each year in between think about what you will need to focus on for that year in order to be one year closer to achieving your vision. Under that heading choose four or five bullet points that explain how that years theme will be realized and that is it. The further out you are thinking, the fewer bullet points you are likely to have.

I use five-year plans for all of my projects and recommend them to all of my clients. They are simple, useable and if written carefully are meaningful, perhaps even more importantly they are easily modified.

Here is an example of the five-year plan for Authentic Business.

2002 – Create

- Define authenticity

- Set up Web site

- Develop mailing list

- Find collaborators

- Win first clients

2003 – Credibility

- Write and publish book

- Define methodology

- Build Authentic Business Guides network in UK

- Initiate Authentic PR

- Initiate Authentic Capital

- Win more clients

2004 – Awareness

- Get on pundit circuit

- Get first international AB Guides

- Start to have Guides supporting Authentic Capital investments

- Develop Authentic Business learning and trading network

- Initiate Authentic Business School

- Write and publish book on Authentic Education

2005 – Influence

- Set up first global Guides and AB network conference

- Create AB change program for corporates and public sector organizations

- Write and publish book on Authentic Government

2006 – Change

- Initiate Authentic Government movement

- Initiate Authentic Education plan

The next step is to share your plans with friends and contacts who can test it for you and contribute to your thinking. Newborn ideas are fragile things and, if this is your authentic business, it will also be deeply personal. When you are looking for people to discuss your thinking with it is important to avoid anyone who will be negative. At this stage you need your confidence built up and negativity will not help.

However, you cannot do this on your own. You need other people's ideas and challenges to grow and substantiate your thinking. Just make sure you choose the right people and brief them carefully about the nature of the feedback you are looking for.

One thing to remember in this process is that this plan is an expression of your authentic self. Therefore you may have to work quite hard at finding a way of expressing it that allows others to become inspired and excited by it.

People are often very wary about telling others of their business ideas and plans. The reason most usually given is to do with fear of the idea being stolen, or intellectual property being compromised. I believe that this danger is far outweighed by the benefits of the input that you gain. If your business idea is truly authentic it is highly unlikely that it will really suit anyone else anyway because it will be the sum of your life to date – which will not be the sum of anyone else's.

Perhaps the real reason that people are so reluctant to share their ideas comes back, again, to confidence. Exposing our dream to the threat of ridicule is hard but, obviously, we cannot admit that our idea might be ridiculous, so we justify our secrecy with a fear of having our ideas stolen.

I am now so used to this method that I find working without feedback a bit like driving in a vast, featureless desert. Without passing features it is very hard to know if you are going the right way or even if you are moving forward at all. As you absorb new ideas and iron out the wrinkles in your plan you can continue to write it down and update your thinking.

At some point you will need to face up to the issue of money. When you first attempt to calculate the costs of starting up you are likely to decide that there are all sorts of things that you need. Business cards, a Web site, a brochure, premises and so on. You may also decide that the way to get these is to start by accessing some money and then using the money to access the things that you need.

Access to funding is very nice and can appear to make things easier. However, it can also be a distraction, and the search for funding can be an excuse for avoiding simply getting on with making an income. Again the reason for this may lie in our lack of self-confidence. Exposing our ideas to the harsh spotlight of actually trying to sell them to someone is a real test of our belief in our thinking.

Newborn ideas are fragile things and, if this is your authentic business, it will also be deeply personal.

There are two solutions to this issue. The first is to morph the planning stage seamlessly into the selling stage so that instead of going to your first prospects with a fully finished offering you go to them with a work in progress and ask them to contribute to its development. As you keep doing this you will be further honing your ideas to a point where they are ready to be bought.

The other solution is simply to avoid spending money and try to keep the business cash flow positive so that you are spending money after you have earned it. If you are starting your business with authenticity you will inspire others and they will want to support you. Their support may take the form of deferred payment for goods or services, or agreeing to some kind of time exchange. Either way, you are freed up to get on with the business.

I know from my own experience that it is easy to convince ourselves that we need props in order to do something. Very often, if you just get on with it, you find that there are many things that you do not really need at all. Understanding the difference between 'nice to haves' and 'must haves' is a crucial distinction.

Over a year after starting Authentic Business I still have no business cards, I simply take cards from others and send them an e-mail when I get home.

SIMPLIFY, SIMPLIFY

'Our lives are frittered away with detail – simplify, simplify'

Anon

It is a crucial component of the whole distraction/capitalist system that as individuals we remain sufficiently confused that we continually buy products in the search for satisfaction/answers/happiness. One of the serendipitous benefits of getting to know yourself and developing self-confidence is that you gain a much better idea of what you need as opposed to what you want. You understand the difference between 'nice to have' and 'must have'.

Knowing your point in life means that you can evaluate decisions on the basis of whether or not they enhance your ability to get to your point, or not. The benefit of this is that you no longer need to earn the money to buy stuff that is ultimately useless to you. The benefit of not needing to earn this money is that it reduces your level of indenture to the system and gives you more freedom of choice.

There is a retrospective element to both of these opportunities as well. For many of us life can be a process of more or less linear accumulation. There are things that pass through our hands but there is a great deal we simply accumulate. There are people who pay for bigger houses and garages (further indenturing themselves) simply to store stuff that they do not use.

In reality, of course, everything is more or less transient, and if we can learn to identify stuff whose usefulness has lapsed and move it on we gain a cascade of benefits.

We have more space to live in. We have more money with which to get the stuff we do need. We satisfy someone else's need thereby reducing demand on global resources.

This is as vital in a business context as it is in a home context as it is in a societal context. How much office space is rented to store useless documents and stuff? If you really must keep it, at least rent some cheap storage rather than using your expensive office space. Then, if you have not accessed it for a year, move it on. At a societal level, how much of our precious non-renewable resources are extracted from the ecosystem and turned into something else which is used for only a few years and then returned to the ecosystem in a far less usable form?

Keeping it moving

We accumulate books and CDs, many of which are precious or frequently used but some are not. I regularly cull my library and sell them on Amazon www.amazon.co.uk or www.amazon.com. Amazon sell listed books and CDs alongside new, so customers looking for a new book or CD are offered the second-hand option at a significant discount over new. Because they would otherwise be buying new the buyers are happy to pay considerably more than you might get at a boot sale.

We also accumulate toys, accessories, computers, cameras, sports gear and so on. E-bay www.ebay.co.uk or www.ebay.com is an ideal place to sell these things and realize cash. There is a huge audience and it is very simple to manage. It is also quite exciting to watch people bidding for things and the price going up.

Other stuff can go to car boot sales, charity shops, recycling or, if it really is useless, it can go to the tip.

TIME AND MOTION

It is not just physical objects that clutter our lives but unnecessary activities and ideas as well. Our time and energy are limited resources; if we are wise we can learn how to use them well and not to waste them.

It is easy to imagine that once some traumatic or uncomfortable event is in the past it has gone and is no longer relevant to your future. It is also tempting to imagine that difficult issues and challenges can be ignored. However, if these things are not properly dealt with they act as emotional anchors, which slow you down and drain your energy.

When no one else is going to challenge you on an issue, it often seems easier to simply bury it and hope that it will go away. Unfortunately this is not what happens. These things gnaw away at our subconscious and come out in some other form. In the long run, as with the physical things, it is far better to keep these things moving than to store them.

Deal with them in your mind, discuss them and, if necessary, take action.

Many of us fill our lives with needless or mindless, activity in order to avoid thinking too much and thereby having to face up to the action that we need to take. Once we are living in authenticity we can easily weed out this activity to focus our time and energy on doing and thinking things that are important to achieving our point.

If you have created a plan using the Post-its, it is very easy to see what are the important activities, the ones you have put in your plan, and what are not. It is also easy to look along your plan, re-evaluate the activities and see if there are any that could be removed. Of course there is always the opportunity to add in new activities that contribute to achieving your point.

As mentioned in 'Action 4: Avoiding distraction and inspiring change' it is also important to be quite clear about the sort of advice and inspiration you want to spend time pursuing. Wherever you seek it – from friends, books or other media – it is important to be selective and focussed about how you interpret the ideas you take in. With practice this becomes easy, but initially it is very hard to sort the golden nuggets from the silt.

Often the most distracting input can be advice from friends. The filter you need to apply is your clear sense of purpose and your values. The difficulty is that your friends, if they are a normal cross section of society, are more likely to have difficulties of their own than to be fully functional and authentic people. The way that this comes out is that their advice, and often their criticism, is centred on themselves and around their own problems and insecurities rather than around your challenges and objectives, even though it may expressed as explicit advice for you.

With friends it is useful to understand that this is where their advice is coming from. Very often friends will be most critical of you for weaknesses they see in themselves. Allow for this and be understanding. The best path, of course, is to seek out those friends who are already functional and authentic and ask advice from them.

Making new friends can be a source of even more objective support and advice than friends you have had for a long time. Before you 'come out' it is often far easier to admit your truths to someone you have known for a short time and with whom you have not built up any myths and baggage than it is to admit these things to friends and family who have known you for years.

FINDING COLLABORATORS

Changing your life or starting a business is not something that you will do on your own. So it is important that you find collaborators. When I started Authentic Business I had around 250 collaborators who contributed ideas and thinking just because I asked them.

Finding collaborators is the inevitable consequence of 'coming out'. Once you are clear and explicit about your purpose, your aims, your values and needs, people will know where you stand and it will be easy for them to see whether you are someone they want to collaborate with or not. Do not be unhappy or spend time worrying about those who you put off by not being vague about your values and intentions – they are not people who you will want to work with in the long run.

One of my main activities these days is seeking collaborators in what I call 'the big project'. 'The big project' is the task of shifting our society from the destructive course we seem to be on to a more constructive one.

Collaborators are people who are naturally on the same path as you are. They are people whose values and intentions are already aligned with yours so that by working together, you contribute as much to their objectives as they do to yours. This is a real advantage for authentic businesses that is simply not available to profit-centric businesses when dealing with customers or suppliers.

Collaborators are people who are naturally on the same path as you are. They are people whose values and intentions are already aligned with yours so that by working together, you contribute as much to their objectives as they do to yours.

Working with Ethical Media and helping them to flourish as a communications design company works as much to achieve my purpose as it does theirs. My purpose is served by the example that Ethical Media set as they become more successful. Their purpose is served by being more successful and helping more positive organizations to succeed. What you might call win-win-win; I win, they win, the wider community wins.

One of the real benefits of working exclusively with collaborators is that it is so much easier than conventional business. In confrontation/exploitation based business you have things like competition, distrust, mutually exclusive objectives, dishonesty and so on. When you are working with collaboration based businesses you can form a mutually supportive team because your objectives are aligned.

When working in collaboration, selling is turned from a process of attempting to convince people that you have the right thing or service for them and competing for each others profit to a process of identifying how you might help each other and accepting when you cannot.

By having a clearly defined and explicit point and telling people about it you give others who believe in the same thing, whether they are explicit about it or not, the opportunity to support you.

By working in an environment where your suppliers, customers, partners, staff and others have an emotional and ideological commitment to your success, it is so much easier to succeed than when the only people likely to benefit from your success are you, the bank and the taxman.

To find your collaborators you will need to be able to articulate your point with great clarity and passion. You will need to do this to a lot of people, in writing, in presentations and in meetings. And most important of all, you will need to listen carefully to the response.

Some people will be cold or even hostile, no matter how well you have expressed yourself. Some will only have their own agenda in mind and will not be prepared to go further. Don't worry about these people.

Others will be interested or even excited. With these people it is important to listen even more carefully, understand and discuss how you might be able to turn that interest into collaborative action. How can you help them? As much as how can they help you?

The collaboration may not happen right away, it may take months or even years but it is important to remember these people and how you can support each other so that when the time comes you can contact them or they will remember to contact you to discuss the specific idea.

When I started Authentic Business I invested months in meetings and conversations. I just kept throwing ideas and conversations up into the air being very clear about what I wanted to achieve. Within six months those conversations started to turn into exciting projects and collaborations.

In order to make that investment of time you will need to have the resources to allow you to spend time and money on getting that message out there. The most vital resources in any enterprise is the energy and motivation to drive it forward and make it happen and the confidence to keep going even when things are looking a bit bleak.

Your energy, motivation and confidence should be taken care of by the fact that this is your life's purpose. I believe that if you are able to commit yourself fully to your enterprise you will have all that you need to make it happen. I am not the first person to have observed this.

> 'Until there is commitment, there is hesitancy, the chance to draw back, always ineffectiveness. Concerning all acts of initiative (and creation), there is one elementary truth, the ignorance of which kills countless ideas and splendid plans: that the moment one definitely commits oneself, then providence moves too. All sorts of things occur to help one that would never otherwise have occurred. A whole stream of events issues forth from the decision, raising in one's favour all manner of unforeseen incidents and meetings and material assistance which no man could have dreamed would have come his way. Whatever you can do or dream you can, begin it. Boldness has genius, power and magic in it. Begin it now!'
>
> *Johann Wolfgang von Goethe*

There is no question in my mind that this is true, both from my own experience and from the experiences of many people I speak to. If you find that it is not true for you it is important that you evaluate what you are doing carefully and see what messages you are getting from the push backs. They will be guiding you towards an easier course.

If it turns out that funding is something you cannot do without, a creative way of approaching the problem is to use the 'Small World Phenomenon', which introduces the idea of six degrees of separation. The idea of six degrees of separation is based on research carried out in the 1960s by Harvard social psychologist, Stanley Milgram. Milgram sent 300 letters to people in Omaha, Nebraska asking them to deliver the letter to a 'target' person in Boston by using personal contacts and then the personal contacts of the personal contacts, and so on to see how many links there would be in the chain. The average number of links in the chain for the 60 letters that arrived was six, hence six degrees of separation. The conclusion is that most people can connect to any other person through around six intermediary relationships. Therefore whoever you need to find is a friend of a friend of a friend of a friend of a friend of a friend.

Make a clear statement about what it is you need and the authentic purpose to which it will be put, which should of course be inspiring. Take your idea and your requirements to a supportive friend and collaborator who you think might know some of the right people. Ask them to recommend you to someone else and tell them about your six degrees challenge.

Meet each person who is recommended to you, tell them your story and ask for their recommendation. If your proposition is good, or gets to be good enough as you develop it with the input from the people you meet, in the end you will meet the right person. Of course it may take more than six degrees but it will be an adventure in any case.

Conventional marketing wisdom is largely about broad casting. If you need to convert ten people you will need to reach one hundred people and to reach one hundred people you will need to be seen by one thousand. This is the product of relatively cheap mass communication media and it is also very wasteful.

Using the six degrees of separation theory is deep casting. Instead of going broad you go deep and, if the theory holds true, you only need to communicate with sixty people to convert ten. For a small fledgling business this is much more manageable. Six degrees is effective in fundraising, in sales and may be useful in other areas too.

DESIGNING YOUR ORGANIZATION

If you are using this book as a linear manual and you have been through the steps discussed so far, you may now be ready to think about the sort of organization you need to achieve all of your objectives – your personal objectives, your relationship objectives and your wider social and environmental objectives.

You may find that you need to invent new ways of doing things rather than simply adopting accepted practice. You want to make a difference, and to try to get a different result by doing things the same way they have been done before will limit your success. What follows is not a formula for organization design but rather a set of challenges to the standard template. The intention is not to explain how to do it but to show that it is worth thinking about alternatives so that the decisions you take are conscious and deliberate rather than just accepting received wisdom without question.

Financial management is often an Achilles heel for idealistic business people. The problem is that there is an almost inevitable correlation between the appointment of a full time accountant and a loss of focus on ideals. It works like this: if you recruit an accountant to a small business they will generally come in at a board level. They will use all of their rational arguments to persuade you and any other board members and slowly, over time, the company will become more and more financially focussed. Outsourcing financial management to a non-executive financial director who only spends a day or two per month on your business is the best way to avoid this unless you are fortunate enough to find a similarly idealistic financial director.

Once a company grows to around 40 people it makes sense to create a 'human resources' function to help in looking after all of those people. When that department is created there is often a temptation to allow them to manage recruitment as well. When this happens and recruitment is taken away from the founders of the company it starts to be based around criteria other than values and instinct. This can lead to a damaging dilution of the energy of the company through the appointment of people who look good on paper but do not share the values and purpose of the rest of the company.

If your business is successful and begins to grow you may find yourself caught in a funding squeeze where you are unable to make the investment required to go further. At this point you may feel that an investor is the right solution for you. If your business is successful, then finding an investor who shares your values will be possible. However, when you do, it is vital to ensure that you and your company have first refusal and a reasonable formula for the investors exit strategy. If the investor is allowed to go to the open market you are highly unlikely to be as lucky with the second investor or the stock financial markets. At the time of writing, summer 2003, I am founding Authentic Capital to address this issue. Authentic Capital will bring together authentic businesses and investors who want to support them within a framework that avoids the business owners from ever having to sell out ideologically.

Teamwork, targets and competition are three accepted staples of business today. I would like to offer an alternative to the accepted view, which may inspire you to be creative in the design of your organization and avoid adopting accepted practice.

Can teams exist in a hierarchy?

A team is a number of people organized to function cooperatively as a group – for instance, the marketing team, the management team, the HR team and so on. In most companies today we are in or surrounded by 'teams'.

It seems this migration from department to team is more optimistic management jargon than descriptive fact. This is not the fault of the people in the 'teams' necessarily, but that of the pervading structure and culture of the company, and of business in general. There is a fundamental mismatch between the formation of teams and the structure and culture of business.

Most businesses are based on hierarchy and individualism. Teams are based on dynamically shifting leadership and a shared aim. In a real team, even one where there is a nominated leader, real leadership will shift automatically and dynamically around the group; think about the way fish shoal or starlings flock, they are not lead by a single individual but leadership shifts rapidly according to circumstance. If they were lead by an individual instead of all turning as one they would all follow in a line as bees do behind their queen. As particular strengths or attributes become important such as skills, knowledge, relationships or location, leadership shifts to where it is most relevant.

In this way a real team has the most appropriate leader for the task most of the time. Conversely in a hierarchy, where there is a single leader most of the time, the 'team' does not have the most appropriate leader. This encourages many of us to question our 'bosses' capabilities and wonder what it was that got them the job in the first place.

The answer to this question is to be found in a wonderful book called *On the Psychology of Military Incompetence* by Norman F Dixon. In the book, Dixon explains how the soldiers most likely to get promoted are the ones who are good at doing what they are told. This is all very well until they get to be generals and there is no one left to tell them what to do except in terms of overall objectives.

Of course, there are certainly circumstances where a single clear leader is appropriate and necessary. This is in very narrow and predictable (or in predictably unpredictable circumstances like on an expedition). Here an individual may be the most appropriate leader for a significant period of time.

For example, Ernest Shackleton, in what is frequently described by historians and leadership experts as the greatest ever feat of leadership, lead all of his men to safety after their ship was crushed by Antarctic ice in 1914. In those specific circumstances, Shackleton remained the most appropriate leader for the group until they reached safety. Under these circumstances, maintaining morale and mutual support was more important than perfect decision making. In fact, many of the decisions made do seem to be illogical and even dangerous looking back from today's perspective, but Shackleton's priority was to maintain belief that they could make it to safety and that positive spirit kept the men moving forwards. Shackleton's brilliance was extremely specialized and, not surprisingly, he never managed to turn it to success in any other walk of life. In addition, the strain of that intense and largely unshared period of leadership probably contributed to his early death.

Shared purpose was probably less of a problem for Shackleton than it is in most business situations today. In meetings we may all sit and agree to a 30% increase in sales targets for the next year, but this agreement does not constitute a shared purpose. In most companies individualism is structural, most incentives are individual, it is individuals that get promoted not teams, it is individuals that get pay rises not teams and so on, yet it is the team that is expected to perform.

We can only give wholehearted commitment when all of our objectives are aligned and our principles are not compromised.

Most of us have very different agendas from the new sales target. We want to change jobs, change companies, go home, write some music, live abroad, be with our family, and so on. You may have been able to change and become your authentic self, but most will still separate themselves into our work self, home self, public self etc. and agreement by work self does not constitute wholehearted commitment.

We also have principles, even the most apparently unprincipled will have areas to which they are not prepared to go. If what we are being asked to do conflicts with deeply held principles, it will diminish our commitment.

We can only give wholehearted commitment when all of our objectives are aligned and our principles are not compromised. 'If achieving that 30% increase in sales means that I can achieve my life's ambition without compromising my principles then I can commit wholeheartedly.'

But this is still not enough to create a team. For a team to exist the objective has to be wholeheartedly committed to by the whole team. For a top performing sports team, winning a race or a match is something that they can all commit to. It delivers on their aligned personal aims. It is very easy to spot when a sports team's aims are not aligned and there is factionalism or individualism – you can see the divergent behaviour and, if they are competing with functional teams, they are likely to loose.

Delivering on sales targets usually only delivers on the aims of the people at the top of the hierarchy, so why would everyone else commit themselves collectively and wholeheartedly to that?

How can you create a team environment in a company?

Again, we have to start with the shared sense of purpose by asking 'what is the point of your organization?'

For a point to be effective it must be systemic in that it needs to involve, engage and deliver for all of the team members to the extent that they hold it as a point of personal, non-negotiable principle, and they trust it absolutely to deliver on their personal life needs as well as team needs.

When you look at authentic businesses you can see that they have a point, which can motivate the individuals and unify them as a group even in tough circumstances.

So, shared purpose is a critical building block, but to actually have a true team requires a real mental shift. Most of us are so culturally indoctrinated with the inevitability of hierarchy that wherever we sit within it, we just assume it is the natural order of things and that there is no alternative.

This is not true.

There are alternatives which we frequently participate in and experience. For example:

- A loving relationship will form a team where each partner leads at their point of strength and there is no hierarchy.

- In many team sports, although there is a nominal captain when actually on the field, the leadership will shift dynamically to where it is most appropriate.

- Many social activities or clubs self manage without hierarchy.

- Dolphins, geese and many other animals perform certain group activities with no hierarchy.

And we can design functional and high performance organization without hierarchy too. In my time at Razorfish one of the striking things was how many high paced Web companies were founded and run by two equal partners, including all of the companies that were bought to make up what became Razorfish. In these cases the lack of hierarchy did not usually spread further than amongst the founders, but in the fast complex world of the dotcom boom two equal leaders were an important advantage enabling the founders to deal with more complexity and breadth. At Ethical Media, we are working with a leadership team of three equal partners and turning that skill base to advantage by enabling dynamic team-based leadership.

Another alternative model is the cooperative. For example Calvert's, a 25-year-old design and print company from South London is a very successful, democratic, non-hierarchical company. Cooperatives are well established and may offer a structure that would suit you, your collaborators and your point.

By early 2003 I was working with five collaborators to expand my company Authentic Business. The basis for expansion is more people acting as guides and working with good companies to help them to become more successful. The basis for expansion will not be a hierarchical structure but rather a flat network structure. Each guide who joins the network will learn the practice of acting as an Authentic Business guide from the collective experience. They will then be free to use the name, the practice and the newsletter to find clients and work with them. There will be a structure for sharing income. Their main obligations to the network will be to maintain its values, to feed back learning and experience and to support the network.

We may decide as a network to contribute to a central fund for collective benefit, such as the running of the Web site. We may also decide to offer a training course to become an Authentic Business guide, but there will be no hierarchy. It is not necessary and is limiting to the individuals and the organization as a whole.

I am also co-founding the 'Creating the World We Want' movement (a movement for the social engagement of all). Again the structure is a totally flat, team-based organization in which everyone will be a leader and there will be no one leader. Leadership will flow dynamically around the organization to where it is most needed, most timely and most effective.

Ultimately, the only thing that prevents us from embracing teams is ego. The challenge, for the strong to let go of the idea of control and the weak to let go of the idea of not having to take responsibility, may be the only real barrier.

What do targets really achieve?

Targets are very fashionable these days. In the UK the government sets targets for just about everything. Schools and school children are constantly set targets and tested on their achievement of them. There are even targets for the results of those tests. Many businesses are based around targets. Targets for growth, share price, sales, costs, even training and personal development.

In most areas the wisdom of targets appears to be accepted without question, as if they are a natural and inevitable part of the world.

They are not.

Like most things, they are optional. They have been designed by our society to give those lacking in self-confidence the illusion of control. They have their benefits, but they also have many, many downsides, and there are alternatives.

The big problem with targets is that they single out and elevate very specific measures of success. At best this leads to very limiting behaviour, a narrowing of potential, and a barrier to innovation; at worst it can encourage creative accounting methods in order to appear to have met the targets, and thereby trigger the reward.

The consequences of narrow measurement can be truly dreadful. It is easy to imagine hospitals turning away seriously sick patients whose operations might fail in order to avoid compromising the success rate target; or specific crop yields targets of intensive monoculture farming being compared to the same crop in mixed farming where the specific crop yield per acre is certainly lower but the overall farm productivity per acre is far higher.

The consequences of targets can also be more unexpected, as illustrated by the story of the very bright thirteen-year-old daughter of a friend of mine who, when asked why she was not studying for an imminent exam, replied that this particular exam was only for the benefit of the school in the schools' league tables and had no benefits for her or her future.

Once again, the fundamental problem is around motivation and alignment. Targets are instruments of control designed to align a divided group of people around simple objectives. The setting of targets is clear evidence that the people taking the decisions lack confidence in their ability to inspire the people involved around a common purpose, and probably lack confidence in the reasons for the action they are asking people to undertake. This may be due to their own inherent lack of confidence in their ability to inspire, their own lack of commitment to the purpose in question or a lack of confidence in the people. The quick fix that is almost universally applied these days seems to be to set targets.

It is certainly true that we need some point in what we do, but this does not have to be articulated in targets. There is a requirement for any business or organization to balance the books and to manage resources towards achieving their point without wastefulness. There is also value in understanding where you are in your journey and where energy is required, which does require measurement of key parameters.

It is the identification of those parameters and the careful interpretation of the results that is important.

The irony of the accepted system, which its proponents would defend to the hilt, is that the measures that are made are so often inaccurate because people are adjusting the figures in an effort to reach targets. Therefore the figures that are used to make rational decisions about how to run businesses are very often flawed.

The big problem with targets is that they single out and elevate very specific measures of success.

When running a business with authenticity we should be confident that the objectives of the participants are sufficiently aligned. There is then little need for targets as a means to measure performance of groups or individuals. Measures are used to understand the dynamics of the situation. The job of decision makers (which might be everyone) within these organizations is to interpret the measures and articulate the requirements they identify in the most inspiring way to the people involved.

By inspiring people and leaving room for latitude and creativity, instead of corralling them with targets, you open the door to innovation and new solutions towards your point rather than towards creative accounting solutions.

COMPETITION

Many businesses would prefer not to have competition, preferring monopoly control of a market. Conventional market economics and societal thinking has it that competition is good because it leads to innovation and it keeps prices low. Unfortunately it also leads to exploitation of suppliers, resources and customers, as well as wasting energy, emotion and time in tactical manoeuvring and deceit. In addition, I would argue that it only leads to innovation and low prices in relation to monopolistic exploitation and not in any absolute sense. Competition-driven innovation is very narrow and mostly defensive – not the kind of creative break-through that we might hope for.

It is competitive markets that sustain our dependence on fossil fuels when it is so obvious that we need an alternative, and those alternatives actually exist. It is defensive competition which leads car manufacturers to continue to pour development into eking a few more years of life out of the internal combustion engine, rather than investing in what would be considered high-risk breakthrough innovations.

In the conventional business model competition is everywhere, if you follow the competitive path not only are you competing with competitors you are also competing with customers and suppliers for their profit in every negotiation.

In his book *No Contest – The Case Against Competition*, Alfie Kohn identifies competition as an activity that is characterized by *mutually exclusive goal attainment* (MEGA):

> 'This means, very simply, that my success requires your failure. Strip away all the assumptions about what competition is supposed to do, all the claims on its behalf that we accept and repeat reflexively. What you have left is the essence of the concept: mutually exclusive goal attainment (MEGA). One person succeeds only if another does not. From this uncluttered perspective, it seems clear right away that something is drastically wrong in such an arrangement. How can we do our best when we are spending our energies trying to make others lose – and fearing that they will make us lose? Most striking of all is the impact of this arrangement on human relationships: a structural incentive to see other people lose cannot help but drive a wedge between us and invite hostility.'

Real innovation is driven by freedom, imagination, confidence and purpose. Leonardo da Vinci was probably the greatest innovator the Western world has ever seen yet who was he competing with? Ironically it was only in the last century that our competition-based society has finally caught up with his free spirited imagination with the realization of manned flight, the development of the parachute and the helicopter which all first appeared in da Vinci's drawings.

It is not innovation itself that is hard to come by. You can easily find brilliant, innovative, world-changing ideas that have been clearly articulated. Just as in da Vinci's day it is the confidence, and consequent ability to implement innovation and turn it into something that is of value to society, that is so hard to find in our free-market, competition-based world.

Most of the innovation that is created by free market economics is directed at ways to liberate rich people from the Northern hemisphere of their cash and pass it on to even richer people from the Northern hemisphere often at the ultimate expense of poor people in the Southern hemisphere. Very little innovation is aimed at the poor, because it is not very profitable to sell stuff to them, they can't pay enough for it.

It may sound utopian, but is some kind of utopia not what we should be aiming for? I believe that if we could align our aims as a society around behaviour and outcomes that are desirable for all of us, and our cohabitants (all living things), competition would be seen to be very primitive behaviour.

Competition is entirely avoidable and only requires two conditions. The first condition is collaboration around a higher aim. The second is the imagination and confidence to offer something different to anyone else. Your authentic business, the business that comes from your heart, the business that is the expression of all of your experience and understanding will inevitably be different from any other business.

People often start businesses with high ideals but find themselves very easily compromised by a tempting contract, difficult trading conditions or their own (or someone else's) lack of confidence. From there they rapidly slide into prostituting themselves and their business to whoever will pay. As soon as the identity and integrity are lost, so is the differentiation and so is the brand, and you have suddenly opened the door to competition.

In setting up and running your authentic business you will face challenges. There will be lucrative temptations, there will be tough times and there will be doubters. What will enable you to succeed ultimately is if you stay true to your values and stick with the dream. That way you will be different and you will have your audience.

THE MEANING OF SUCCESS

What is success? What does it mean for you? Since you are reading this book presumably you have already eliminated ego props as definitions of success like flash cars and jewellery?

When I was at Razorfish and we were furiously recruiting the brightest and most creative people we could find, I would ask candidates for their manifesto rather than their CV. I thought that having a future that was aligned was more interesting than a past that ticked a few boxes. These days when people ask me for advice, I suggest they write the profile they would like to see written about themselves in a favourite magazine in ten or fifteen years time.

If writing is not your thing, perhaps you could draw a picture or compose some music. The important thing is that you understand it and can interpret it. Don't think about it too much and over analyse it. Just sit down and do it.

What would your life look and feel like if you were living your dream? What would others say about you? What would you say? Where would you be? Who would be with you? What would you have around you? How would you spend your time and your energy? How would your needs be fulfilled?

Success is very individual. It is not about impressing others, which only causes tension and is illusory. It is about satisfying your own functional (as opposed to dysfunctional) needs while living within your functional values. However, it is possible to find collaborators whose aims are sufficiently aligned to create a business which delivers on both your personal and collective interpretations of success.

Once you have begun to define it, you may find that it is achievable from where you are; it may be that with a shift of perspective you can discover the success that you already are.

We have a great tendency to over-elaborate our interpretation of success to include all sorts of things which, in reality, have little value or meaning to us. Real multidimensional success is far simpler than that. It involves feeling happy, safe, comfortable and fulfilled, and having time to enjoy yourself. This does not need to involve highly paid jobs, multiple cars or houses, expensive holidays or clothes. Allow yourself to think of success in simple, personal terms rather than in competitive, egotistic terms.

When I ask people what success means to them they often ask it back to me. And my answer is peace. Peace from inner conflict and doubt. Peace from external friction and conflict, and peace amongst all of the creatures of our universe. This may not be as ambitions and utopian as it seems. There is no doubt that there is a connection between our state of mind and our interpretation of the world around us.

Remember reality is subjective, if we are paranoid or easily worried we are likely to see conspiracy and threat at every turn. In *A Beautiful Mind*, Russell Crowe plays a brilliant mathematician in the US during the Cold War. His paranoid delusions, combined with the drugs used to treat him, nearly destroy his life, until he decides to take control and just live consciously with the delusions.

If we are confident and assured these conspiracies and worries do not even occur to us. Confidence is about knowing that you can deal with situations as they occur. In a previous life I raced cars – I now see it as my version of going to university. It took three years, saddled me with some debts, I had a great time and learned a lot. One observation given to me by a former Grand Prix driver was that as drivers got better, so their horizon moved closer.

The very best drivers would only be focussing a few metres ahead, confident their reactions were so good and so fast that they could cope with whatever happened and still deliver on their overall plan for the race.

So when you are looking for signs of success, look on the inside and to your closest collaborators. Do not be distracted by the external pressures of marketing or society. If success for you is caring for orphans in Laos, make a plan and go and do it. You will not get a second chance.

If you are working within your functional, authentic self, your contribution to your loved ones, your community, our society and our cohabitants on this planet will far outweigh the costs of having you here. And if our race is to continue to have a place on this planet, we will all have to contribute more than we take out.

Those Who Are Already Doing It 4

In this section we will be looking at a number of existing authentic businesses. I have chosen mostly consumer businesses rather than business to business companies because they are better known and it is easier for readers to be customers and support these companies.

The businesses are all successful in that they exist and the people involved believe passionately in them and are happy. In no cases have I asked for profit and turnover figures as you will not decide to have your authentic business because of the potential profit or revenue, although some were given. As Maria from Organic Express puts it: 'Profit is a like breathing you have to do it, but it is not what gets you out of bed in the morning.'

In each case I visited or met key people who felt very passionately about the company and have asked the questions below from a fairly sceptical point of view. We have taken these questions as a jumping off point and have used them to explore other areas of interest.

- What is the point of the business?

- How do you go about achieving that point?

- What are the values of the business, how explicit are they, and how do they influence the day-to-day work of regular staff?

- What do you believe the business and other advantages and disadvantages are of your attitude to business?

- Apart from profit, what other measures of success do you have and how do you measure them?

- What challenges to do you face in sticking to your values?

There are many more authentic businesses in both consumer and business sectors and I will be writing more case studies on them over the coming months on the authentic business Web site www.authenticbusiness.co.uk.

The businesses are:

- Organic Express

- Yeo Valley

- innocent

- Howies

- Solar Century

- Cafédirect

ORGANIC EXPRESS

Organic Express is a catering company working from London that provides beautifully prepared and delicious food for events, from conferences to weddings. The founders, Maria Clancy and John Kavaliauskas, had virtually no background in catering before setting up Organic Express, but agreed they had had one disappointing conference lunch too many, where the catering failed to respect the context of the event and, whether through its flavour or its ethical baggage, it had a diminishing effect on the event. They decided to make a difference by setting up Organic Express.

My interview was with Maria and we met at the predictably delightful Konditor and Cook café at the Young Vic on The Cut near Waterloo Station. Waterloo was my choice because that's where my train home leaves from. Konditor and Cook was Maria's suggestion because the food is good, which is, as became clear in the interview, something Maria really cares about. She could also park right outside. This might sound a little less than idealistic until you realize that Maria drives an electric car.

My first question is to ask what is the point of Organic Express?

Maria immediately connects food – the basic stuff of life – with the entire web of humanity, linking the micro with the macro in a single sweep.

> *'Organic Express was set up to reflect the symbolic value of food. Where it's going, what it means, how it gets to you – it's how you create a food business that has meaning.'*

Maria's response to a question about the values of the business, how explicit they are and how they affect the people in the business is interesting; she says that they really have not spent a great deal of time thinking about their values, they 'just live it'.

Maria makes it clear that Organic Express cares about all of the implications of the food they serve. They insist on it being organic, they ensure it has been fairly traded (and are constantly seeking more fair trade products to incorporate into their range), and they also seek to minimize the 'food miles' that have been invested in your lunch. While this does involve extra work they do not have an alternative because this is who they are. Feeding people great food is a powerful way to connect with them. At each event Organic Express caters for, they have a communication station where they are able to engage with participants about the symbolic values of the food they are consuming, specifically organic farming, fair trade and food miles. It's clear that passion and caring are also very important values to Organic Express.

With much of their work being for ethically orientated organizations such as Body Shop, St Luke's Communications and Human Rights Watch, Organic Express offers a tangible expression of the ethics and values of the organization at their events, which contributes rather than detracts from the message of the event.

This synergy is powerful at supporting the messages of both host and caterer. When else have you ever heard of the caterer routinely being given the opportunity to address the guests at an event? It is a regular feature of events for Organic Express and a reflection of the power afforded the participants by collaborating towards a higher overall objective.

I then asked how their values affect the day-to-day work of the staff. Maria's response was that they feel like the luckiest people on the planet because their head chef is Carolyn Robb, who was previously head chef for the Prince of Wales. Again, Maria's values are so intrinsic to her that she is hardly aware that she has them, but clearly attracting the best people and valuing them highly is important to her and to the business. The challenge she does identify is that, as the company grows, they may have to be more explicit about their values to ensure that new staff understand them and share their commitment so that they too can engage with the issues.

The really big advantage to running a highly ethical, value-driven business is that the work has meaning and value in a wider context than just something to do. This is incredibly motivating for herself, for John, for their staff and for their customers and suppliers. Maria says that if the business were not run this way she would not be doing it. She sees no disadvantages in being highly ethical, but it is a challenge. The fact that the infrastructure for organic fair trade catering is nothing like as well established as the infrastructure for intensively farmed, exploitative catering does mean more 'leg work', as she puts it.

Organic Express currently have no systems in place for measuring success, apart from profit, but they are very keen to measure the impact of their pound as it flows through their suppliers and the positive ripples it can make.

The really big advantage to running a highly ethical, value-driven business is that the work has meaning and value in a wider context than just something to do.

The final question was to ask what challenges they face in sticking to their values? Maria's answer: 'None. The values are the foundation of the business and it would be meaningless to do anything else.'

Organic Express is a young company making its way in a sector in which ethics and values are often in short supply. Their natural constituency of ethical businesses, social NGOs, networks and enlightened individuals have embraced them as a hungry child holds an apple. The more marginal market of the fashion conscious corporate and government departments have also latched onto the benefits of having great food and being appropriately 'green'.

We can only hope that in a few years time organic food and catering is so plentiful that it ceases to be a differentiator. In the mean time Organic Express will flourish as values of excellent food without exploitation sets them apart from the rest of the sector.

YEO VALLEY

Yeo Valley is the second largest manufacturer of yoghurt and yoghurt products, fulfilling 18% of the UK market. The company is based on the northern slopes of the Mendips above Blagdon Lake in Somerset. Their offices are in a beautifully converted hotel with wonderful views across the lake.

Yeo Valley is a family business, Tim Mead is the chief executive, and his mum looks after the cows; and the cows are central to Yeo Valley, they feature on and in nearly all of their products – just have a look at the packaging. They are pedigree Friesians and look bigger and shinier and healthier than any other cows you have ever seen and that really sums up Yeo Valley. At Yeo Valley they care about everything and the result is a big, shiny, healthy business and cows.

The offices are attractive and calm, their machinery is state of the art, their cows are wonderful and they care for the dry stone walls and the hedgerows and the wildlife.

I heard a man singing in the corridor and calling out to people as he passed their offices, then he burst into the reception area where I was waiting. This was Tim – CEO and majority owner of a group of companies employing 850 people. As he introduced himself he exuded energy and we positively bounced into the café-style meeting room.

Dan Rusga, one of the marketing team, who brought the interesting perspective of having worked for Diageo until about 18 months ago, joined us. At a recent reunion Dan had trouble convincing some of his former colleagues of just how good life at Yeo Valley is.

One of the first things you notice at Yeo Valley is the attention to detail. Everything is immaculate and well thought through and this is obvious to a first time visitor to their head office. Tim confirms this: he believes that every area of the business is an opportunity for excellence and an opportunity to be better than the competition.

However, Tim's definition of 'everything' goes far further than most business leaders. At Yeo Valley they take enormous care of their hedgerows, their dry stone walls, their ponds, their wild life, their cows and their people (the accident rate in their facilities is 75% below the industry average), and you can taste the results of this care in the yoghurt.

Tim sees the point of Yeo Valley as a challenge. The challenge is to prove that you can build a company up to be a major industry player and a self perpetuating enterprise without selling out, either literally or ideologically. You would have to say they are a considerable distance down this route. They are certainly a major player and not only do they retain ownership but they have no borrowings, having been able to pay back earlier loans from retained profits.

This financial security gives Yeo Valley enormous autonomy in their decision making. It allows them to choose to focus on the areas that they know are vital for the long-term security and success of the company and community even if they do not offer short-term returns. In an industry dense with consolidation, losses and factory closures, this is a remarkable achievement, which receives little coverage in a business press that is so focussed on public companies.

Part of the attention to detail is avoiding wasting money. Dan explains that there is a family attitude to saving money. Unlike previous jobs where people would routinely stay away at expensive hotels for extra nights and each take individual cars, at Yeo Valley people take it upon themselves to avoid unnecessary expense.

One of the things that Tim is very conscious of in other businesses is the kind of silo-based factionalism where departments feel that they are competing for resources and recognition. In Tim's view this leads to damaging and wasteful self-aggrandizement and protectionism. Departments can easily get into trying to spend more money to justify their existence and then having to work harder to justify the extra spending in a vicious circle.

The Yeo Valley response to this is to have an aligned and trusted workforce who aim for a shared objective rather than personal or departmental glory.

And part of Tim's job is managing the balance between departments and not allowing some part of the company to run away with things. Working to maintain a low staff turnover and not bouncing people around the company is crucial to this as it allows people to develop relationships skills, trust and intuition about their tasks.

Yeo Valley are very conscious to avoid complacency. They have a strong market position and it would be all to easy to let things slip. The buzzword for 2003 is simplicity. As Tim says 'It is easy, as you grow, to allow things to become complicated – like in the decision making process – decisions here get made very quickly without endless reports and focus groups and consultants.'

'It is not so much the quality of decision but the enthusiasm with which it is carried out that makes the difference', says Tim. With that attitude from the CEO it is no surprise that people at all levels feel confident enough to take responsibility for their actions and decisions.

> *'It is not so much the quality of decision but the enthusiasm with which it is carried out that makes the difference'*
> Tim Mead, Yeo Valley

What Tim and Dan are saying is that these values of care and commitment are shared by the entire work-force from the dairy to the boardroom. Pride, passion and care are evident in all sections of the business. People understand the part they play in the business as a whole and caring and quality encourages caring and quality.

Having established the best service levels and the best products in the industry, people are reluctant to let the company and their colleagues down. It is a recognized phenomenon that people are less likely to litter in areas that are kept clean and tidy. The same, it seems, is true in a more general sense. You can foster a sense of exemplary behaviour by behaving in an exemplary way, it certainly seems to work at Yeo Valley.

I asked Tim what the advantages and disadvantages of doing business in this way were. 'Life is to enjoy and to spend 30 years doing something you do not enjoy is a waste of a life.' He remembered, from his time as an accountant in the city, people having two coats so that they could leave one on the back of their chair so that people would not think they had gone home before 10pm. 'What is the point in that?' he asked.

'Whatever you are doing has to be inspiring, our business has to be enjoyable for all so that they choose to do it. Otherwise there is no point. If commercial pressures force you to run the business in a way that you do not agree with, you like to think that you would walk away. But you do have responsibilities.' And there is the rub.

If things start to go wrong, do you focus in on what you know and what makes you different and special or do you give up your differentiation and go the way of the market?

Is it more responsible towards your workforce to tough it out with your individual approach even when things get hard, or is it better to drop the profit-related bonuses, make people redundant, stop maintaining the hedges and walls, let the machinery age, basically to cut costs for short-term gain? If the time comes, perhaps that is a question best answered by the workforce themselves.

In the end Tim says, 'You have to believe that behaving badly towards people and the environment is likely to become a significant commercial risk and those who are socially and environmentally responsible are likely to be at an advantage.' It is certainly possible to use marketing to overcome a lack of substance and integrity. Many companies manage to fool a lot of the people for a long time but you have to hope that eventually having integrity pays off.

I asked Tim about how they measure their performance. After a long pause he replied, rather enigmatically, 'QSPPP'. Fortunately he went on to explain.

QSPPP stands for Quality, Service, People, Plant and Profit – in that order.

- *Quality* – the quality of products is based on your own opinion and on feed-back from customers. Quality elsewhere is based on a gut feel of how good things are in the company.

- *Service* – levels are set for each part of the business; interestingly this applies both to external customers and when dealing internally with other parts of the company. I get the feeling this is no box checking exercise – that would not be the Yeo Valley style – more a set of principles that are understood, even if they are rarely articulated.

- *People* – Yeo Valley puts a lot of time and effort into people. There are frequent reviews and training, and an induction process for recruits that lasts for a week.

Yeo Valley are also keen to recruit the best people, believing that if you recruit someone at a 20% lower salary they might be less that half as good as someone for 20% more. That extra 20% might be worth a great deal more in savings and revenue every year.

- *Plant* – Yeo Valley are big believers in investment in first class facilities, which are efficient and up to date. While the cash flow side of the business is kept tight, the capital side of the business benefits with constant input. If you avoid spending £150 on a hotel for the night you can spend it on your own place and continue to enjoy the benefit.

- *Profit* – Profit has to be part of the system because it ensures survival, but it is also crucial that it does not become the overall driving force.

I guess the last word on the Yeo Valley commitment to purpose should be that they have changed the memorandum and articles of association for the organic business so that the main purpose of the business is not just to make profit but to grow the organic market and profit as an outcome.

Yeo Valley is a truly inspiring company – significant and profitable – which sees caring as an integral part of their success. Not just caring about profit, but caring about people, wildlife, customers and suppliers, the environment and the cows. They prove absolutely that if you stick to a few principles, some generic and some your own, it is possible to build a thriving business in a highly competitive sector without selling out either financially or ideologically.

INNOCENT

innocent make smoothies, thickies and juices. The company was founded when three friends felt the strain of living and working in London getting on top of them. To validate their belief in the market they ran a novel piece of research, buying £500 worth of fruit, juicing it and taking a stall at a music festival. They put out two bins for the empties under a sign saying 'Should we give up our day jobs?' The bins were marked 'yes' and 'no'.

Legend has it that by the end of the day the 'yes' bin was overflowing while the 'no' bin only had a couple of bottles (put there by their mums in a desperate bid to persuade them to stay with their 'proper jobs').

innocent are based in a fairly nondescript business park in Shepherds Bush, West London. The usual mix of small businesses, such as a locksmith, a recording studio and some people who make rowing machines inhabits the rest of the business park. innocent is immediately obvious because there is a van dressed up as a cow outside. The van is painted black and white and sports eyelashes on the headlights, horns on the roof, udders at the back and large bovine ears attached to the mirrors.

There are, apparently, three entrances, the roller shutter door beloved of business parks, the regular door and the window. Above the roller shutter is a sign saying 'Cows', above the door one saying 'People'. The sign above the window says 'Burglars'.

You walk into an empty hall and then in to an equally people-free kitchen. On one wall is a pin board smothered in messages from delighted customers, pictures sent in by bored office workers (one of the sections on the Web site invites bored office workers to contact innocent) and letters from Prince Charles and the House of Commons. On another wall are a set of open cubicles. Each cubicle has a forename under it and each one has a plate, bowl, mug, knife, fork and so on neatly stacked inside. I am immediately struck by this neat solution to the perennial small business washing up problem.

Through a door you walk into a large open office where everyone works. Here I met with Dan. Dan is innocent's Brand Guardian and copywriter and so I hold him largely responsible for all of the little jokes on the bottles and the two neat little books that innocent have published. One is the amusing company rule book and the other is a fun and useful health book.

We sit in another part of the large open room where the floor is covered in Astro-Turf, huge beanbags and a sofa. On the other side is a fully equipped kitchen where the prototype juices and smoothies are formulated and tested by willing volunteers (the staff).

Dan explains that when they came up with the idea the founders were all busy types with lots of parties and bars to go to. They worked as management consultants and in advertising, enjoying their jobs but ultimately feeling that they wanted to do something for themselves. Eventually it dawned on them that all of this working and partying was not really respecting their bodies and that they really should try to do something a bit healthy. They knew that fruit was really important but it was not always convenient or cool to eat an apple.

They looked at the other options and found them frighteningly full of unnatural additives and other worrying things so they started to make juices and smoothies without any additives. They felt that they already knew their target market (people just like themselves, too busy to think about their health all of the time) and so pressed ahead with trying to come up with drinks that tasted good, and that also provided people with their recommended daily intake of fruit in a bottle. After much trial, error and naysaying from 'experts', they came up with some tasty recipes

In the long run, sticking to the point has served innocent well. They now make a range of fabulous drinks that defy most of the industry standards – their shelf life is too short, they need to be chilled and they are too expensive. But still customers and, importantly, retailers love them.

Top of the list of values at innocent is being natural. Natural applies not just to their juices but to the people as well. Staff are expected to bring their whole selves to work and not to put on any special performance. Saying what you think and feel is part of the job.

innocent make a real point of encouraging a direct relationship with their consumers, which is very unusual for a manufacturing company. The number for the 'banana phone' is advertised and customers are invited to call it if they have any complaints, questions, or if they are just bored. The 'banana phone' exists and it is in the main office and not on any particular persons desk. The idea is that everyone is responsible for answering it and everyone should participate in the relationship with consumers.

One of the key measures of success within the company is whether staff leave. So far only one has and that was to have a baby (good excuse). Using abstract, outcome-based measures is an interesting model for performance indicators. I guess if you took a really rational approach to 'not having staff leave' you could simply shackle them in with 'golden handcuffs' so that leaving was a very difficult option. This is not the innocent model.

The innocent model is to look after staff and to make their daily lives fun and rewarding in more ways that the purely financial. Staff are able to feel that their daily work is not only contributing to the health of their customers, but also to the well-being of others. innocent donate a percentage of their profits to impoverished farmers in India, the money pays for the planting of mango trees and the purchasing of cows via an NGO called Women for Sustainable Development. Thus innocent contribute to their suppliers' lives as well. Next step, providing a scholarship for someone to go and work out in India and help the mango/cow projects become even more effective.

The innocent approach to a mature and highly competitive overall drinks market has been to carve out a brand new niche in which they are the unquestioned leaders. The charm with which they have imbued their brand and the thoroughness with which they have applied it; vans, AstroTurf, jokes on bottles and so on, has won innocent awards and loyal customers as well as a huge amount of publicity and consequent awareness. This combination of great products, savvy marketing and direct relationships with customers has contributed to innocent being able to develop very positive relations with the big supermarkets which must be the envy of many other suppliers.

HOWIES

Howies is a clothing company based in Cardigan in West Wales. Amongst their customer base of mountain and BMX bikers and skateboarders they are revered for their uncompromising attitude to life and ethics. For example their clothes are produced in 'happy' factories from organic cotton, because globally more pesticides are used in cotton production than food. And Howies are not fans of pesticide use.

Howies started out as a part-time, sitting room based operation for copywriter, Dave Hieatt, and his partner Clare. While he was working for big London advertising agencies during the day, and struggling with the ethics of the clients he was promoting, Dave was dreaming up slogans and printing them on T-shirts by night. One of the early classics was the T-shirt with a dollar laminated onto the front and the word slave printed underneath. Perhaps an indication of how Dave himself was feeling at the time. Howies defy the rest of the clothing industries obsession with disposable fashion by being extremely well made, in classic designs that are not intended to go out of fashion.

I arrived just after the big spring delivery, so there were T-shirts, bikes and old wardrobes everywhere. The old wardrobes were part of an award winning point-of-sale promotion. Howies invited artists to decorate the wardrobes using various sociopolitical themes. Some of the wardrobes have been on tour to Japan.

The current home for Howies is a rather disappointing standard industrial unit on an estate on the outskirts of Cardigan. But Howies flight from London, and being full time, is a relatively recent move and what might be their new offices and much, much more is a beautiful old mill a little closer to town.

I met Dave at their unit and we inspected the new deliveries, including a rather surprising T-shirt with 'I ♥ GM' on it, which seems very un-Howies until you notice the third sleeve. Other products promote cycling – a courier bag with a 'pass on the right' arrow on the back another comparing the number of bikes with the number of cars you can fit in car parking space. Other T-shirts focus on the importance of getting out there and enjoying your life rather than spending all your time at work.

Dave's last job lasted just 12 weeks before he realized that he simply could not do this stuff any more. So with a partner he set up a subversive marketing agency called Anticorp. In spite of the name and an aggressive attitude to corporate policy and behaviour Anticorp was successful – with corporates. Although he was now able to do the work very much his own way he was still promoting things he could not believe in. The only solution was for Howies to become full time.

The point of Howies is to be provocative and to get people thinking about global issues and their lives and to ask some pretty deep questions. And all of this is achieved through the medium of T-shirts. Howies do it all with a subversive charm and humour which is irresistible to their audience of cyclists and skateboarders, young people who want to state their opinions against the establishment.

Dave seems genuinely astonished when he says 'some people don't think about these global issues'. 'Can you imagine having a friend with no point of view?' he asks. For Dave one of the big benefits of increased sales is that by selling more T-shirts they are getting more people to talk. The Howies approach avoids being worthy or campaigning, preferring to engage with their customers' own humour and desire for individuality. The result is that Howies get sent Christmas cards, biscuits – in effect 'fan' mail, customers saying thank you. 'This gives you are real sense that you are doing something', says Dave.

Howies products are made to very high standards, in terms of materials used, working conditions and craftsmanship. In an industry renowned for using sweatshop labour and shoddy materials to drive prices down and margins up, this makes Howies products seem expensive, especially to retailers used to selling £15 T-shirts with a 60% margin. This is why Howies retailers are known as believers. Believers are those who understand that it is not just about short-term profiteering at the expense of others but that there is actually a bigger picture. When I met Dave he had just turned away the biggest order they had ever received, because the retailer concerned was making conditions that would compromise Howies values and standards and that to Howies is not an option.

There is a wider point here as well. How is it that we have become conditioned to stratospheric and continually rising property prices where one of the most basic human requirements can easily take up 50–60% of your income and yet we also expect other staples such as food and clothing to be cheap and to get cheaper. Cheaper food and clothing almost inevitably means that someone is being exploited. When you see a T-shirt for sale for £10 remember that the retailer probably gets £5 the tax man £1.75, £0.50 for transport, the distributor will take around £2.50 leaving £0.25 for the manufacturer. If we are ever to live sustainably we are going to have to get used to the idea that things that deplete global resources will be a great deal more expensive than things which are produced sustainably.

This price challenge means that a good deal of Howies sales are direct through the catalogue and the Web site and plans for their new base include the building of their own shop/café/cool place of inspiration. The catalogue is a mini masterpiece in its own right. It is the only catalogue that I have ever read from cover to cover. At the time of my visit the new catalogue was being finalized. One memorable page had a list of things that Cardigan is without such as McDonald's, Pizza Hut, a big supermarket and so on, at the end of the list it simply says 'Oh Well'.

The catalogue integrates products with inspiring messages and ideas, such as using reply-paid junk mail to send your junk – such as an old bath – back to the junk mailer at their expense. The resulting catalogue is something to keep, refer to and talk about with your friends. Exactly as intended. The catalogue and the Web site also have a library of the books that Howies find most inspiring. If you request one Howies will send it to you and ask that you return it when you are done, a practice that will be expanded with the opening of their own shop. The proof of the effectiveness of such practices is that Howies routinely get a 20% response rate from their catalogue when industry norms are closer to 6%.

As far as Howies are concerned, ideas are the most important thing in the world and they do not conform to nine-to-five. For ideas to occur there needs to be challenge,

motivation and inspiration and it is difficult to get those three if you are doing the same thing day after day. Howies want to get more ideas everywhere; in the factories, in the warehouse, in the deliveries. Dave says 'we want to make it more electric with people coming up with new ideas everywhere.'
This is what keeps the company fresh and keeps people coming to work.

The point of Howies is to be provocative and to get people thinking about global issues and their lives and to ask some pretty deep questions.

Like most small business people Dave finds himself head of finance one day and head of T-shirt packing the next. In a business that is so clearly based on creativity and ideas it is easy to be distracted by the day-to-day and making time to come up with new ideas is a real discipline. Dave seems to achieve this through his deeply held belief in what they are doing and by engaging with the community that they have created.

Dave is inspired by an advert for Burton Snowboards, which asks 'Will you still be doing it when it is no longer cool?' He asks the question of himself 'it's like organic cotton – will you still be doing it?' Howies is not built on fashion and, whilst it may have moments of being in fashion, it is not what drives the company or seemingly those who have invested in Howies.

As with many of the businesses I spoke to, Howies put a great deal of emphasis on their people. One of the challenges Dave makes to the company is to say 'its all very well you working for Howies but how is Howies going to work for you?' One way in which Howies hopes to answer this question is through the institution of 'too nice to work days'.

One of the fundamental problems of growth in any business is that as they grow they lose touch with the roots that inspired them in the first place. For Howies their roots are in mountain biking and skateboarding. If they do not get out there boarding and biking regularly they will lose touch. And that is why everyone who works there is encouraged to make the most of 'too nice to work days' and get out on their bikes or boards when things are not too busy.

I asked Dave about the disadvantages of working this way. He identified margins as a challenge but then said 'we do not know any other way so we don't have the alternative of falling back on conventional business wisdom'.

Dave relates a story from *The Art of War* by Sun Tzu. A leader with a hundred men who has to fight a force of a thousand marches the men in to a dead end valley when asked by one of his men why he chose to go there he replied 'because there is no way back'.

You get the feeling that there are no true measures for success at Howies but what they want to know is how much debate they can create, how much innovation, how many awards they can win and how much press coverage they can get as the third biggest clothing company in Cardigan Bay. Dave believes that if they are being interesting and attracting interest then they must be doing something right.

One thing Dave is really certain of is that he would rather Howies was influential than big. Staying independent is a vital factor, as soon as you start selling out financially you end up having to compromise and end up selling out ideologically as well. Howies has investors but they are in it for the long term and understand the values of the brand. 'They will get a financial return in the long term' insists Dave. I believe they will and they will get a great deal more along the way as well.

SOLAR CENTURY

Solar Century is an energy company —one of the UK's leading suppliers of systems that turn sunlight into electricity. They design and install systems for businesses and homes, which make use of sunlight and new legislation to generate energy and sell it back into the grid as well as powering the building of which they are a part.

You find their offices between the hustle and bustle of the market stalls just behind Waterloo Station and enter a sleek, calm entrance hall. Upstairs is a large reception room, which is lined with displays of varying types of solar system. I am meeting Joy

Green, who is one of the marketing team and has been at Solar Century for several years and has watched and participated in its growth.

Solar Century believes in profits with a purpose and they have a big purpose to drive them and their profits, and to unite a diverse team. The purpose is to make a big difference in the fight against global warming and in creating a cleaner environment by revolutionizing the energy and construction markets. The team to do it includes a variety of backgrounds – from city suits, the military, oil companies and Greenpeace activists. You might imagine tensions between these extremes but it seems that purpose, the strong social and ethical values of the company and its people-centric approach help everyone to recognize each others value and collaborate.

The values here run deep, Solar Century works, as far as possible, with an environmental supply chain, preferring to collaborate with independent and ethical suppliers. For example Solar Century won't sell cadmium telluride-based systems because of the long-term environmental problems that cadmium causes, so at the moment their focus is on silicon-based systems. Joy admits that they would have to do some pretty hard thinking if technical developments meant that cadmium telluride-systems became significantly cheaper or higher performance than silicon. Which would create an uncomfortable tension between their desire to see solar proliferate and their environmental values. This risk means that promoting the development of silicon-based systems is an important part of Solar Century's role.

Many staff cycle to work and there is no car park or company cars to put in it. Solar Century encourage visitors and staff to use trains where possible, which is supported by their location immediately beside Waterloo Station. Working with clients who are not supportive of Solar Century's values is an issue and is discussed, one of their agreed working principles is that they 'will not do business with those who oppose change'. It is much more about getting people to engage constructively rather than use solar as a 'greenwash' to help tick a few CSR (Corporate Social Responsibility) boxes.

Solar Century has been instrumental in working for the big shift in thinking which has been able to get people to accept that solar power can work in the UK. One aspect of this has been their work with RIBA (Royal Institute of British Architects) developing course work for their CPD courses (Continuing Professional Development) for architects, which encourages them to think about practical and architectural use of solar applications. Another aspect has been government lobbying which has been successful in winning the significant current grants policy that is encouraging the construction industry to think and use solar.

Solar Century believes in profits with a purpose and they have a big purpose to drive them and their profits, and to unite a diverse team. The purpose is to make a big difference in the fight against global warming and in creating a cleaner environment by revolutionizing the energy and construction markets.

So far in the domestic market, housing associations lead the way with innovative thinking aimed at generating power and reducing long-term costs. Developers are being motivated by changes in legislation but are less open to innovation. In the commercial market, again, the public sector leads the way at the moment, but companies are beginning to take an interest after a few early projects that had more to do with PR than principles.

It seems ironic that such a small independent company should find itself shouldering so much of the responsibility for what should be considered to be such an important social and ecological task. When founder, Jeremy Legget, started his mission he did try to get the oil companies to go solar but they had very little interest in changing the status quo. The oil companies attitude is to let the small players grow the market and take the risks and then buy their way in when there is little risk left to take.

As we have seen over and over again selling out is the death of idealism. The long-term success of the purpose of Solar Century and other authentic business relies on those taking decisions holding the values and using those values to evaluate their decisions. Selling out control financially means selling out idealistically. If that seems likely to impede growth and limit success in achieving our purpose we must think carefully and be creative about how we achieve the growth without selling out. If it is the right thing to do there is always a way.

For Solar Century those values are: to be positive, courageous and lead by example. If we are positive, courageous and prepared to lead by example, it must be possible to find a way to grow the business and to become a powerful force for change in the energy and construction industry globally without selling out.

Solar power is a 'leapfrog' technology in that, like mobile telephones, it can be installed in areas that have no existing service, without the need to go through the previous phase. In the case of electricity this means no need for centralized, power station-based generation, and no extensive grid of pylons, substations and power lines. In this way, energy systems can be installed for rural communities at a fraction of the cost of more mechanical infrastructure. Solar Century have committed a percentage of their profits and energy to enabling such systems in developing countries when they are cash positive.

It is this sort of positive connection with the world and the obvious opportunity for reducing our society's dependence on fossil fuels, with all of the social, political and environmental trauma that this has lead to, that the people who work at Solar Century find so inspiring, and makes them proud to tell friends about what they do. This inspiration is coupled with a people-centred approach that sees a responsibility roster for team meetings. Whoever's turn it is to take the team meeting is responsible for the content and agenda, which may be work related or may focus on some other issue that is important to them.

The board makes decisions in the company but everyone outside the board can get their ideas and feelings put forward for inclusion in board meeting discussions. There is also a very open and flat structure that makes directors easily accessible to all staff.

The advantages of working in these ways are that people like to work here and are happy to stay late and commit their energy, precisely because they are not working for a big soulless corporation. There is also tremendous support from other stakeholders – like customers and suppliers who feel that they are collaborating with each other rather than competing for each other's profit when they are negotiating.

There is even collaboration with other players in the alternative energy market as they work together to grow the market.

The disadvantage is that it is all very new ground, not just in terms of the technology but also in the behaviour of the business and so it takes a great deal of confidence to stick with it, particularly when there are people offering to invest, which might resolve immediate challenges but compromise the long-term purpose.

However, Solar Century have a great deal to boost their confidence in their belief that they are heading in the right direction. Their measures of success include: the falling price of solar modules, the improving perception of solar energy, an increase in the understanding of climate change, and the tone and spread of the debate. In all of these areas it is clear that Solar Century are being tremendously successful.

CAFÉDIRECT

Following the collapse in coffee prices, which led to the end of the International Coffee Agreement (ICA), Cafédirect was formed to help strengthen the influence, income and security of coffee growers in developing countries and to link them directly to the consumer in the West. It was founded by Oxfam Trading, Traidcraft, Equal Exchange and Twin Trading in 1991.

Cafédirect, which actually existed before Fairtrade was an established concept and organization, was influential in setting the criteria, which are today's accepted international standards. In addition to paying Fairtrade price minima, Cafédirect has its own 'Gold Standard' – a guarantee to always pay above the world market prices and to support the growers through major tailor-made 'Producer Support & Development' programmes. This ensures the farmers benefit from a decent income to cover their production costs at the very least, and the opportunity for them to develop their business and support their families and communities.

Cafédirect's offices are in an attractive little mews area at the end of Old Street on the very edge of the City of London. Here, I met Chief Executive Penny Newman – a veteran of The Body Shop.

Once we had the obligatory coffee sorted out, a cafetière of the lovely premium Cafédirect Organic Macchu Pichu, I asked Penny about 'the point' of Cafédirect. She told me that its aim is to be a 'mainstream brand which proves you can trade successfully in a competitive market helping producers in developing countries get the correct price for their goods to provide a sustainable livelihood while providing customers with fantastic hot drinks.'

The great news, Penny believes, is that both ends of the supply chain benefit from this way of doing business. The growers get a fair price for their hard work and the consumers get a better beverage because the growers give Cafédirect the pick of the crop. She hopes that Cafédirect's success can set an example to other companies – it is not only a profitable way to do business but also one which offers significant and specific social advantages.

There is still a perception in the industry and among consumers that Cafédirect is niche but, as the sixth largest coffee brand in the UK, that view is seriously out of date.

Penny is unapologetic about the need to be profitable. 'Without profit, we are not sustainable ourselves – we end up being niche and charitable.' Unlike conventional business models, where supplier and buyer are pitted against each other competing for each others profits, Cafédirect producers are keen to support the company in making profit as it demonstrates to other brands that they can make money without exploiting growers too.

It was hard getting started, because Cafédirect was new to the industry and wanted to do things differently. Penny relates the story of having to persuade a roaster to clean out an entire roaster so the Fairtrade beans would not get mixed with others. That seems reasonable except that Cafédirect only had ten tonnes of coffee to roast and a roasting order is normally hundreds of tonnes without the need to specially clean out the roaster. The roaster supported them and now the volumes are much more commercial and the roasters are now taking a serious interest in Fairtrade.

There is still a perception in the industry and among consumers that Cafédirect is niche but, as the sixth largest coffee brand in the UK, that view is seriously out of date. This position has been achieved in only 12 years, displacing many older and more established brands, and they are on course to become the fifth largest.

Following the success of Cafédirect, Teadirect was launched and is now the fastest growing tea brand in the UK. All of this has been achieved with a small marketing spend and no TV advertising. They even hear anecdotally that Nestlé is beginning to see them as a competitor.

The figures are impressive and should challenge the preconceptions of those who believe that profit is only available to those who are aggressive, hard and exploitative. The latest figures show a 20% sales growth, enabling over £2 million to be paid in premiums to growers and a further £300,000 to be invested in 'Producer Support and Development' programmes – and still make a profit. This success, and the confidence that it brings in its approach, makes the whole team even more motivated and determined to be pioneering and innovating. Penny says: 'Everyone cares in the company – they are super-motivated because they know that selling more coffee means more money and more support for more growers.'

At this stage in Cafédirect's development, Penny believes that focus on the company's objectives, ensuring that everything is aligned around the mission, is their priority. While they are growing at such a rate, the risks are more around dilution of energy and loss of direction than being caught out by competitive pressures. She is dismissive of imposed measures such as CSR (Corporate Social Responsibility). 'CSR is only about reputation and how it affects the bottom line. Cafédirect is about ethics and values – these are part of our DNA.'

Those values are embodied in the company's 'Gold Standard' policy. 'Everyone is involved and we want people to express and live them for themselves rather than impose them on people.' Penny sees a significant part of her job as coaching the team to share and live their own interpretation of the values on a daily basis. From that range of personally held values comes a common purpose. The 'Gold Standard' is derived from that common purpose and creates a set of policies which act as a framework which people can express themselves within.

Unsurprisingly, Penny sees these values and policies as significant advantages. 'We are unique, which gives us an edge, seeing the impact of our work really encourages and motivates you. And when you hear stories about the way businesses are eroding societies you realize that you could not work any other way.' Penny has never been interested in being conventional anyway and has always wanted to do things the way she thought they should be done rather than simply following convention. She went to Body Shop thinking she was going to learn retail but actually learnt a whole new way of doing business. Very few companies give people the time and the space to find themselves but they did at Body Shop and they do at Cafédirect.

This unconventionality extends into the measures which Cafédirect uses to judge their success. They look at things like how much income goes back to the producers and what percentage that should be of turnover, the number of producers and their families they are helping, the tonnage of coffee they are selling, and how they balance where it gets bought from to encourage the maximum independence among the growers.

Other measures are connected with the work on the ground. Last year 10% of profit went to special projects in the growing areas, such as helping farms convert to organic or helping with skills development. However, not everything is measured, the approach is for the team to agree the sorts of outcomes they are looking for and they just know if it feels right. For example, significant effort goes into spreading learning from one area to another so that farmers can benefit from each other's learning. This is not measured but the results certainly feel right.

Part of the success is the wider success of suppliers in selling more of their products – ideally to other Fairtrade outfits. 'We don't want to end up with a monopoly on any of our suppliers.' However, with some farmers selling 50% to Cafédirect and 50% to the regular market and still making a loss, there must be a concern that one of the outcomes of Fairtrade is to subsidize even lower prices for the rest of the coffee market.

Cafédirect see themselves as an infinity symbol. A permanent double loop that links coffee drinkers to growers, with Cafédirect in a connecting role sharing learning between growers, passing money from consumers to growers and creating awareness of growers amongst consumers.

Whilst they are enjoying great success, challenges remain. Trying to raise investment money from people who have the same values is a real problem when you have absolutely no intention of allowing the business to sell out ideologically. But Penny is really motivated to show that it can work. Another challenge is managing growth at 20% plus without compromising values and the culture clashes that these values can provoke when dealing with other companies. For example, the deal that was done with Costa Coffee, after two years of discussion, to get the brand explicitly there as a partner not just as a supplier. And a major supermarket's offer to run a 'buy one, get one free' promotion is not understanding how it would devalue the brand to present it in this way.

... the move from 'worthy' to 'lifestyle' brand, focusing on top quality hot drinks with no bitter ethical aftertaste, has been accomplished with spectacular success ...

Cafédirect is hard to sell to a conservative and profit-led industry. It is easier to sell to the very PR conscious big supermarkets, but the independent retailers remain sceptical. However, the move from 'worthy' to 'lifestyle' brand, focusing on top quality hot drinks with no bitter ethical aftertaste, has been accomplished with spectacular success, and with such commitment it is easy to envision a real change in how hot beverages are made and sold.

Reading list

These are a selection of books that inspired my thinking. Some are referenced in the text others have just been influential.

- *Ishmael, My Ishmael and The Story of B*, by Daniel Quinn. Reading Ishmael really encouraged me to look at the world differently and to keep asking questions.

- *The Alchemist*, by Paul Coelho, reminded me that I already have what I am searching for and the best place to start looking is inside.

- *And We Are Doing It*, by JT Ross Jackson, helped me to understand the nature of the system and that there are alternatives.

- *Hitch Hikers Guide to the Galaxy*, by Douglas Adams, covers just about everything

- *Perfect Health*, by Deepak Chopra, helped me to understand that my health is my responsibility and my problem.

- *Optimum Sports Nutrition*, by Dr Michael Colgan. All of the nutrition education I should have had at school.

- *The Invitation* by Oriah Mountain Dreamer, check with yourself and see how you are doing.

- *Jonathan Livingston Seagull*, by Richard Bach. The nature of conformity and the battle for individuality.

- *The Great Food Gamble*, by John Humphrys. Clarity on where our food comes from and the true price we pay for it.

- *On the Psychology of Military Incompetence*, by Norman F Dixon. Explains the limitations of the hierarchical system in which we live.

About Authentic Business

Authentic Business exists to demonstrate to the business world at large that GOOD business is good BUSINESS. We believe that business founded on a deeply held positive purpose has fundamental commercial advantages over business whose primary purpose is profit.

One of the ways in which Authentic Business does this is through the service of Authentic Business Guides. Guides work with you and your business to guide you on the journey towards your goal. Strengthening your confidence in yourself and your values and helping you to achieve your purpose.

Any journey is about travelling from one point to another. Authentic Business Guides can help you to understand your starting point, your destination, the route you need to travel in between and the key identifiers that will help you to know if you are travelling in the right direction and at the right speed. They can also help you develop the skills you might need along the way.

- We will start by developing your understanding of your present situation and if necessary helping you to create a stable and secure platform from which to move forward.

- If you have not already articulated it we will then work with you to identify and explain 'the point' of your business. You need to be able to explain why your business exists and is important to the world because it is very demotivating to be pointless.

- We will then create a very simple five-year plan that will help you and your team to focus your energies on the immediate priorities and build your success.

- We will then focus in on the first phase and identify all of the tasks that need to be accomplished, who is responsible for their delivery and when they need to be delivered.

For more information contact neil@authenticbusiness.co.uk

Index